Getting Started with the Bible

CW00952392

Getting Started with the Bible

A Guide for Complete Beginners

John Holdsworth

CANTERBURY
PRESS
Norwich

© John Holdsworth 2007

First published in 2007 by the Canterbury Press Norwich
(a publishing imprint of Hymns Ancient & Modern Limited,
a registered charity)
13–17 Long Lane, London EC1A 9PN

www.scm-canterburypress.co.uk

British Library Cataloguing in Publication data

A catalogue record for this book is available
from the British Library

ISBN 978-1-85311-846-3

Typeset by Regent Typesetting, London
Printed and bound by
CPI Bookmarque, Croydon, CR0 4TD

Contents

Preface

Writing a book like this gives me opportunity to thank, in a general kind of way, all those parishioners, congregations, trainees and students who have taught me over the years that if I am to be any use at all in my job I must make the Bible accessible. I am grateful, more specifically, to SCM-Canterbury Press, and especially to Christine Smith for her faith in the venture. Thanks are also due to colleagues with whom various bits of the project have been discussed, especially Leslie Francis in Bangor and John Watt in Cardiff. Bishop Carl Cooper has been a constant source of support and encouragement. Most of all I am grateful for the tolerance of my wife Sue and my immediate family during a very busy period that has seen the birth of our first granddaughter. She will be part of a generation for whom the community's story will not, naturally, be told in religious terms. If she and her contemporaries are ever to open the Bible, their interest must first be aroused; and they must be taught by the kind of people for whom this book is intended: curious people, with a deep interest in the world in all its variety, and a vestigial sense that faith might still have a vital part to play. And so I dedicate this book to her:

Mia Grace Barnett
Gyda chariad

Introduction

What was that all about?

When I was a curate on a large housing estate in south Wales, I once organized a community service in the church. (This was the 1970s after all.) I asked a teacher from one of the local schools if she would be prepared to read a lesson and she readily agreed. No, she didn't need me to turn up with the reading for her. She would bring her own Bible. The reading I had chosen (for some reason that now completely eludes me) was 1 John 2.9–14. On the night, at the appropriate moment she ascended the lectern and began. But something was dreadfully wrong. Instead of reading from the first letter of John (1 John), she began reading from the Gospel of John (John). It began in the middle of the account of the marriage at Cana and ended virtually in mid-sentence, in the account of Jesus cleansing the Temple. What would parents and citizens make of a teacher who could make such an obvious mistake and read something that made absolutely no sense? I was incredibly embarrassed for her. Later that evening, I had to come to terms with an even more awful reality. No one had noticed. I trace my own curiosity about public Bible reading to that point. But are we any better now at making sense of the Bible when we hear it read?

The combination of new lectionaries and new liturgies means that people are now having to make some response to hearing bits of the Bible they never knew existed. There is something vaguely uncomfortable, I feel, about listening to some Old Testament tale of genocide, slaughter, human sacrifice and pillage, without turning a hair, only to be told at the end: 'This is the word of the Lord.' And something even worse about having to say: 'Thanks be to God.' Do we hear what we are saying? Have we just concluded that it doesn't really matter? Perhaps we think that the reading of the Bible is essentially a private thing and perhaps the renewed interest in Bible courses is evidence of that. No nurture course or process evangelism course is complete without a substantial Bible component. But what about people who do not want to attend such a course for whatever reason? Is there not a reasonable expectation that Sunday worship should itself have a nurture and process evangelism component? Is that not why we used to read the Bible in public in the first place?

And if those of us who regularly hear the Bible read in public have ceased to care about whether that reading has any sense or purpose, what right have we to inflict it on others? My heart often goes out to those who attend weddings or funerals according to a Christian Order of Service. More often that not (and especially in funerals) the families have an idea of what they want the service to say, and a degree of bespoke creativity is usually encouraged. But when it comes to choosing a Bible reading, often without any commentary from the officiant, a completely discordant note can be struck. A family that has chosen readings such as 'Stop all the Clocks', 'Do Not Stand at my Grave and Weep', or 'Death is Nothing at all', can be completely nonplussed by hearing a passage from Paul's Letters to the Romans or Corinthians. What has that got to do with anything?

And so I was prompted to write this book, initially as a kind of punters' guide to the Bible. I had particular people in mind. They might be busy people, people who don't want to be patronized and people who do want to recapture the sense of the Sunday service being a nurturing occasion. They are people who want to use their minds, who don't want a party line, who do want to relate their listening to the Bible to their contemporary experience. And they may be people who are puzzled about the relevance of the Bible anyway. What I wanted to provide was a framework of understanding, which would allow some-one to listen to a Bible reading, locate it in a particular way, and be able to use it as a means of reflection on experience. In the process I wanted something that might help, in some small way, to rehabilitate the Bible as well.

Although I began with that audience in mind, it soon became apparent that this by no means exhausts the categories of reader who might welcome such a book as this. It may be that those who want a relatively brief overview as a precursor to embark-ing on a more detailed course might find this useful. I hope it may also be of help to those lay or occasional ministers, readers and speakers whose training has not covered every single corner of the Scriptures, and who might like a first-aid post to give some indication of the way to approach a specific, unfamiliar book. But in particular, I have come to appreciate that there is a whole generation of Christians who have not necessarily come to faith with much Bible contact; and that, I think, is something relatively new. It is not necessarily a bad thing. After all, being a Christian is not fundamentally about believing lots of doctrines, or knowing lots of things about how religion operates. It's about a relationship with God and wanting, however we might describe it, to be a follower of Jesus. But there comes a point where Christians have always found that relationship needs to be nourished through Bible reflection, and fewer people today than would once have been the case feel equipped for that. The book aims to be a resource for them.

Alongside all that, I wanted to make the point that new intro-ductions to the Bible should be written fairly regularly in order to keep up with the amazing pace of scholarship in biblical disciplines. This is not a book that could have been written 20, 30 or even ten years ago. It is a book for now, that wants to take readers into the confidence of scholars and encourage Bible study as some kind of joint enterprise between the two.

I have divided the Bible contents into sections that make sense to me, paying particular attention to the bits you are most likely to hear. Each chapter is headed 'Getting Started on . . .'. There is an initial section of description, followed by a section setting out what we need to know to make sense of the kind of material under discussion. A final section will suggest ways that portions of text can be pastorally and practically useful in understanding the Christian enterprise better. The hope is that this will provide the beginnings of a link between the text and experience. It will be less of a blueprint than a road-map, offering different routes, and indeed different destinations.

There are three introductory chapters ('Before Getting Started'), dealing with questions that a first-time reader might want to ask, and the kind of answers to some of them that Bible scholars have reached at this point. The first asks, why be bothered to read it at all? The second gives a whirlwind tour of the Bible to describe its contents in one narrative, and the third asks, what is the Bible about? Hopefully all three chapters will give an opportunity to think about what the Bible is, and the sense in which it could be described as holy or sacred literature. I think the book works best if you start at the beginning and read through it in order, but see what works for you. Wherever you start you are unlikely to do worse than that poor teacher in South Wales.

Part One

Before Getting Started

I

Am I Bothered?

Why should anyone bother to read the Bible? It isn't as if it's a book that is easy to read. It doesn't have an index. The contents page simply lists a set of titles, which at first sight mean nothing at all. Is it, you wonder, like a novel that has to be read from the beginning to make any sense of the plot? Or is it more like a reference work that you dip into to find the bit of information you want? What does it mean to call it, the *holy* Bible? How does this book differ from other books?

Reflection

I heard of a teacher in what used to be called a teacher training college who began his course on the Bible in the very first session by silently entering the room, taking a Bible, and setting fire to it (before dowsing it in a carefully prepared bucket of water). The rest of the session was spent in a discussion of how people felt about that and why. Most felt uneasy, not just because the idea of burning books was so abhorrent, but because burning this book had special significance.

How would you feel if you witnessed the burning of a Bible in circumstances like these? What does that tell you about your approach to the Bible?

God's Good Book?

Clearly some people think it is very important to be able to read the Bible, and to do so with understanding. Most services in

Christian churches include some reading from it, usually in short sections. At the end of the reading there is often a declaration: 'This is the word of the Lord!' What does that mean? Most Christians certainly would want to say that the Bible is the word of God, but they would not say that he had somehow dictated it. In fact, it was written by dozens of different people, few of whom knew each other or ever believed that they were contributing to something that would one day be the holy book of a third of the world's population. These people wrote over a very long period of time. The oldest portions of the Bible date to perhaps the tenth century BCE. The newest date from perhaps as late as 130 CE. As you might expect, writings from diverse backgrounds and circumstances, with many different authors' styles and genres, show few obvious signs of coherence. And certainly anyone approaching the book with a view to finding moral guidance would have to look very hard indeed in the first instance.

This so-called 'good book' contains many tales of genocide, double-dealing, looting, pillage and disaster, apparently sanctioned by God. It has very few passages dedicated to life coaching as such, and those that it does have give permission, for example, for parents in some circumstances to kill their children. This legal direction is mixed in with rules for dealing with what to eat and how to kill it, when you can have sex, and how to cope with menstruating women; all three of which our society has probably resolved quite adequately, without resort to religion. In so far as the Bible is a moral guide for Christians, its ethics are a matter of debate and interpretation in trying to trace the principles and lines of ethical thought that underlie particular rules made in a time and culture far removed from our own.

When Christians ask, 'Why have a holy book?' they cannot rely on the answer, 'Because God dictated it as the authoritative guide to life.' It is not God's text message to a distant world. It might be better to describe it as a record from a number of people who feel that they have had a significant experience of God. These experiences have come in a variety of ways and circumstances, which the subsequent community of faith has decided are authentic. The Bible describes a people trying to understand God better, firm in the belief that a relationship with him lies at the heart of meaning in life. The Bible is a list of the clues they've found about who God is and how he acts, which they want to hand on. The most revealing clue of all is the whole phenomenon of Jesus of Nazareth. The writer of one New Testament letter sums up this view when he says: 'In many and various ways God spoke of old to our fathers by the prophets; but in these last days he has spoken to us by a Son' (Hebrews 1.1). All other Christian beliefs and practices derive from understandings of who God is and how he acts. This is called theology.

Inspired authority

Often, people try to describe what is special about the Bible by saying that it is *inspired*. People sometimes struggle to find the words to express a deep feeling that what they are reading is the authentic word of God. Inspiration becomes a way of describing how God involves people, and speaks through people – people who perhaps did not recognize the significance of what they were writing. In the case of the Bible writers, God himself is in some sense claimed as the one who invests the material with its inspired quality. How this works is no easier to demonstrate than any other kind of inspiration.

Reflection

We often talk about something or someone being inspired, to point to something quite surprisingly special. In retrospect, we speak about literary works being inspired, to describe the way in which some books continue to have meaning way beyond the original author's lifetime, or perhaps have a continuing capacity to change us. Often readers nowadays find in some historic works, such as the writings of Shakespeare, meanings that the authors themselves never even dreamed of. Often these are profound works that explore aspects of the human condition, and whose authors appear to have special insight.

Have you ever used the word 'inspired?' What were the circumstances?

Can you think of any book that has led you to think of it as inspired, or which has inspired you to new understandings about life? What was the book and what did it do for you? How did you view the author as a result? Does thinking about this help you to see the Bible in a different light?

For Christians, to say that the Bible is the word of God, is also a way of saying that it carries authority. There is no copyright on the word 'Christian'. Any group can claim to be Christian, no matter how bizarre their beliefs and practice. There has to be some way of setting out what authentic Christian belief and practice looks like, and some standard you can refer to. This was a particular problem in the early Church when Christianity was very new and there were lots of different understandings of what it was all about. The books we call the New Testament were written from the midst of arguments and discussions about what Christians should believe and how they should organize themselves and behave. In subsequent centuries there have been lots of differences of opinion on every aspect of Christianity, and the Bible is a reference point for the arguments of all points of view.

Unity and diversity

In so far as the Bible has become the standard authority for Christians throughout the world, what the Bible says matters enormously, and influences the cultures of entire nations and even superpowers. The problem is that there is no one way of reading it that is acknowledged by everyone to be legitimate. Some people do read the Bible as if they were reading the Highway Code, able to ignore the massive cultural divide between the times it describes and the here and now; to read a set of rules that is valid for our society as it might have been for desert nomads with no fridges. Others want to ask questions about why different books were written. What were the concerns that prompted them and what are the agendas that are driving them? They want to learn from all that scholarship can provide, about the sources and history of the text, about ancient literary forms of writing and about the social setting of writers and audiences. They want to identify the questions about God that prompted these works, and to see if they bear any relation to questions raised in communities of faith nowadays. They see ambiguity in the texts, with many different layers of meaning.

These different ways of regarding and reading the Bible are poles apart, and are responsible for some of the polarization in the worldwide Christian community on questions such as, for example, the place of homosexuals in church and society, the abortion debate, capital punishment and the place of women in church and society. Sometimes these views are described as 'traditional' and 'liberal', but that is quite misleading because one of the unresolved issues is precisely about how to interpret the traditions.

Reflection

Imagine being part of a group that is trying to discern a biblical way to make a decision about, say, whether cohabitation is permissible before marriage. Here is a summary of some of the contributions.

- *In the Bible marriage is clearly set out as the norm for sexual relations. Nothing else should be considered.*
- *What the Bible describes as marriage isn't what we know as marriage now.*
- *The Bible was written at a time when only men were considered important. We can't read anything from a situation like that.*
- *Jesus taught love above all things. He would not want legal-*

istic rules to get in the way of a developing authentic relation-ship.

Do you identify with any of these positions? Would you take a completely different view? How helpful do you think it is to refer to the Bible when considering contemporary questions of this sort?

Editing the Bible

To view the Bible as a record of religious experience is not to say that all experience of God stopped somewhere around 1,900 years ago. But clearly it would not be possible to keep on adding books all the time. Reflections on the life, ministry and death of Jesus from those who were affected by them first, surely form an appropriate place to stop. Neither is it to say that these documents are the only ones that describe that kind of thing. So we might well ask, why just have these books in the Bible, and who chose them and why? The answer is not straightforward.

The contents of the *Old Testament* were not chosen by Christians but by adherents of the Jewish faith, for whom this remains a sacred text. The Old Testament is the name Christians give to a collection that the Jewish faithful know as 'Torah, Prophets and Writings'. That title is a description of the contents in their three original categories. The Torah books are the first five in the Old Testament. The word Torah is not easy to translate. Sometimes it is translated 'law', and elsewhere, 'teaching'. Essentially, it represents the foundation documents of the Jewish religion, and so speaks of beginnings, fundamentals, identity, basic understandings, and shared vision. The Prophets section includes a larger number of books. Some of these, like the section from Joshua through to 2 Kings, look more like history than anything else. Others, like the book of Jeremiah, combine some story-telling or narrative with long speeches. Yet others, like Isaiah, have the speeches without the narrative. We do not know how these particular books were chosen, or exactly when; but they were regarded as authoritative during Jesus' lifetime, as the Gospels record him as referring sometimes to 'the law and the prophets'. The third section or 'writings' were the last to be added. Ancient traditions tell us that these books were chosen by a group of Jewish scholars at the very end of the first century CE. This means that the last books of the Old Testament were not finalized until after most of the books of the New Testament had been written. If that isn't odd, what is? Christians adopted the Greek translation of the Hebrew scriptures, which puts the books in a different order, and groups them according to their supposed content. That is the order in which we find them in our Bibles. There are four categories: law, history, wisdom and prophecy. Changing the order does have an effect on how we understand them. We shall look at what is involved later in the book.

Canons and Councils

The exact contents of the *New Testament* were only finally agreed by a Christian Council that met in the fourth century CE, although there was broad agreement about most of it much earlier than that, and certainly during the second century. There was never much disagreement about the four Gospels, or about most of the letters attributed to Paul. Most controversial were some of the shorter letters attributed to John, James, Peter or Jude. Some books, which are not part of our Bible, such as the second-century 'Shepherd of Hermas', were hopeful for a place, but ultimately failed to get in, though we can still read them in other collections. What those early Christians were looking for, were books that had been used and accepted in churches all over the (known) world: books which they believed could be authenticated by tracing them back perhaps even to the apostles themselves. Nowadays, scholars would be less certain about how possible that is.

The most basic point to emerge from this is that the contents of the Bible were chosen by the community of faith, whether

Jewish or Christian, who considered them significant, worth holding on to, worth passing on. The word sometimes used to describe the contents of the Bible is 'canon', the name given to the yardstick with which a soldier's pace is measured. Judge for yourself how appropriate that is, but it gives an insight into the minds of those responsible in the various Councils for providing the finished product.

Testaments

Then you might want to ask, why are there two testaments? Christians, as their name suggests, are followers of Christ. They have a special interest in those documents in the Bible that speak about him. But he himself was part of a tradition, and much of what he said makes little sense if you're not aware of that tradition. The vocabulary, the idioms and the assumptions he can take for granted in talking about God, all have a history. To put it another way, Jesus enters the story of God at a particular point, and the authors or editors take for granted the fact that everyone else has read the story so far. The word 'testament' means agreement or covenant, and the particular titles given to the different parts, Old Testament and New Testament, reflect the Christian belief that the arrival of Jesus takes the story of God in a new direction, such that what people understood by God and his relationship with humankind before Jesus' time could truly be called 'old', and what they would understand about God and that relationship as a result of Jesus' activity could truly be called 'new'.

Experience

The Bible is used today both by those who have a strong sense of God's presence, and those who want to find out why he seems absent in their lives and experience. It provides a means of *checking authenticity*. When is an experience a religious experience, and when is it little more than a sentimental warm indulgent feeling? From the Bible, Christians can see in a variety of ways that a truly Christian religious experience is one that at least:

- challenges your assumptions
- leads to real change
- reaffirms you as you
- widens the horizons of what is possible or imaginable
- devalues selfishness
- puts us on the side of the weak and oppressed rather than the strong and the oppressor.

This kind of checking is not done quickly or with the use of an index, or by turning to the right section, or by referring just to some words of Jesus or a prophet. It is a sophisticated task, which includes reference to a wide variety of biblical sources – stories, poems, speeches, sermons – all of which authenticate each other.

The Bible is used by Christians to *reflect on experience*. The kinds of question Christians ask that involve this kind of reflection are, among many others:

- Where is God in all this?
- What am I called to be and do?
- How can I make a difference in this situation?
- How can I act to make things better here?
- How can I exercise my citizenship responsibly?
- Why is this happening to me?

It will be one of the tasks of this book to involve readers in reflective tasks with biblical text. One of the ways in which this can be done with the Bible is by *finding ourselves in the story*. And that in turn means finding a way of reading the texts that enables that to happen. The Bible, for Christians, is not just a book about long ago. It describes life situations in a way that enables us to identify with them, but we have to feel our way into the text first.

Tradition and communities

Christians read the Bible because *it describes the early traditions of the faith*. For a religion that puts a huge premium on the gathered community, the Bible tells us about the possibilities and pitfalls of forming a religious community such as a Church. The community of faith has a key role, as we have seen, in determining the contents of the Bible; but the Bible has a key role in determining the faith and order of the Church. The Old Testament describes various kinds of religious community. There is the family or household, the tribe (whatever that means exactly), the priestly communities that formed around the king and the court, the communities that formed around some of the prophets and perhaps were responsible for remembering their message. There are models of community for settled times and for troubled times, for times when the community feels under siege and when it is relaxed and careless, when the community is a majority and when it is a minority, when it has power and when it is powerless, when it is settled and when it is wandering. The New Testament is said to contain more than 90 pictures of the new religious community that results from Jesus' teaching. Some are used quite often like 'kingdom of God', or 'Body of Christ'. Some are used only once, in stories of Jesus or illustrations from other Christian writers. Clearly there is a huge but fascinating task in deciding which model is appropriate for which setting. In so far as the Bible is the book of the Church, it both defines the Church and is defined by it.

Reflection

So we might think of the Bible as:

- *checking authenticity*
- *helping us to reflect on experience*
- *placing us in the story*
- *connecting us with the Church's traditions.*

Which of these is most important for you? Which, if any, would

persuade you 'to be bothered' to read the Bible? From the
preceding paragraphs has any phrase or idea struck you particu-
larly? You might like to share that with other group members,
or reflect further on it yourself.

Skilled labour?

What resources, or what skills do we require, to access the
message of the Bible in a way that is legitimate and that will help
it to be for us what we want it to be?

It is perhaps worth reflecting that for most of the last 1,900
years, most of those who have claimed to be Christians have
been unable to read the Bible at all. Even after printing presses
were invented and developed, most people's knowledge of the
Scriptures would come via the church expert, in sermons and
perhaps in some remembered passages. This was true until
recently in our own culture and remains true elsewhere. And
those church experts depended in turn on experts in academic
life. Even after most people could own and read a Bible for themselves, few had the confidence to read it without the help of
experts.

We got into this situation almost by accident. About 250
years ago, at the beginning of the so-called Age of Reason,
Christians felt that their faith was under threat from a new
breed of scientific academics. These were people who sneered at
the categories of faith. They demanded, rather, examples of
evidence, in the absence of which religion was regarded as little
more than primitive superstition. Christians wanted religion to
have an honoured place in the world of academic study, and
insisted that it could be studied as other subjects were. The
question was: with what critical tools do you study it? Do you
use the tools used by students of history, or those used by
people who study literature? However it happened, it was the
former path that won out. And so the Bible was studied as a
series of historic texts. This meant that the study attempted to
answers to questions like:

- How did these texts develop and how were the books formed?
- On the basis of what the texts say, how can we learn more about the events of those days long ago?
- What did the people believe in those days?
- What kind of religious institutions did they have?

That sort of study assumed that finding out about the truth contained in the texts, finding out what their message is, meant asking and answering those questions – all of them based on the fundamental question: What really happened? So in order to get at the truth you needed experts who could tell you about the text: people who had studied ancient history and anthropology.

Unskilled labour?

More recently, scholars have begun to work at the alternative approach and to use the critical tools available to students of literature. This has changed the emphasis altogether. To discover the truth contained in a piece of literature you don't need to be guided by an expert. You need rather to think about the effect that the writing has had on you. Now, that is not to say that looking at the texts as historical documents is useless. It has told us a great deal about the setting of the books and the issues they describe. But if we think about them just as history, we shall have quite a narrow view of the Bible.

- If we are only interested in what actually happened long ago, then we are bound to get bogged down in fruitless argument about whether the world was really made in six days, or whether Jesus' miracles were possible.
- We might be tempted to think we shall know more about God by finding the sites of places and events described in the Bible, or that arguments about faith are really arguments about available evidence.
- If we read the Bible as a plain record of fact, we soon find ourselves embarrassed by having to explain the ethnic cleansing

described in the Old Testament, and again we spend fruitless time arguing about the meaning of, for example, the virgin birth or resurrection.

- We lose the opportunity to explore the creative genius of biblical writers.
- We read sophisticated arguments as if they were facts, and take no account of creative literary devices, such as the use of irony.
- The whole thing seems remote. Something happened a long time ago. People from those long ago days said that something (the end of the age) would happen a long time hence, but what's happening now? It's all a bit like Alice in Wonderland's jam yesterday and jam tomorrow but never jam today.

The skill of reading books

Some of the results of historical scholarship are very useful, but in order to access the truth of the Scriptures you need more than that: you need the ability to read a book. What skills do you need to read a book with understanding? We might think of the following.

A phrase used by drama critics is equally applicable to other forms of literature, namely, '*the willing suspension of disbelief*'. In other words, say you were reading *Animal Farm* by George Orwell, you wouldn't dismiss the book by saying, 'this is stupid because horses can't speak and pigs don't dress up'. You would accept that the point of the story does not depend on things being factually true or even possible.

That means you would be able to identify satire when you see it, or to recognize when an author is using irony. You would accept and learn about the *particular style and conventions employed* by an author. We shall see this point being made in the Bible itself. At several points in John's Gospel Jesus says things that are meant to be interpreted in a sophisticated, poetic or spiritual way, but which are taken by his hearers at face value. They are effectively lampooned for this.

Reading literature with understanding means accepting that in some sense *you are in the hands of the author* – a skilled practitioner – who is able to lead you, persuade you, even manipulate your feelings by various means. This is particularly true when the author has a point to make and an argument to win.

Reading literature works best when *the reader gets involved* in the whole thing and interacts with it, by wanting to solve the mystery or by identifying with one of the characters. It is this kind of involvement that usually leads to a positive judgement about a book such as, 'it moved me', or, 'it upset me'.

Read 📖 *John 3.1–12 and John 8.12–30*

Here are a couple of examples of Jesus' words being understood in the wrong way, because they have been taken too literally, and the hearers are made to appear stupid as a result. Can you think of instances where you have misunderstood or been misunderstood in the same way? Some people think that we may have been guilty of something similar with regard to the whole Bible! Can you think of any one place where you would like to see some reinterpretation that would take the argument in a different direction?

Fact and fiction

These are arguments for introducing a new perspective and not for abandoning historical enquiry altogether. Christians firmly believe in the historical reality of Jesus, and the reality of his suffering, for example. The Bible is not a work of fiction in the same way *Animal Farm* is. However, even factual writing employs literary skills, and perhaps especially so when, as in the case of the Bible, authors are trying to win an argument.

What kind of historical skills are useful in today's climate of enquiry? We still want to know when books were written and what prompted them to be written, and what questions were being asked, to which biblical texts might have been thought to provide answers. We want to know what effects they had on real people in real life. We would like to know more about the readers, and their setting. To what extent did the audience determine the way the message was presented? Historical enquiry of various kinds is helping us to have a broader picture and to provide some answers, as we shall see. However, scholars are now far less inclined than they once were, to regard the Bible books as history pure and simple, containing a reliable record of fact.

If we are to get the most out of reading the Bible then we need some *literary resources*, some *historical help*, and we need to be a little *self-aware*. That is, we need to recognize from what perspective we are reading the text and what it is doing to us. Also, we need to have *a sense of our own wider context* if we are going to be successful at making connections between the text and our own experience, because at the end of the day the world is what the Bible is about, and is the main focus of God's interest. What kind of world do we live in? What makes our community tick? How does our political system work? What are the trends in our society and what makes for change? What makes us anxious? What fulfils or ruins our lives?

Grand designs

If we were setting out to design a religion and to write its holy book from scratch, we wouldn't end up with either Christianity or the Bible. The religion would be far more predictable. Rules would be clear. God would never be frustrated. Good people would invariably be rewarded and evil people punished. Bit by bit the world would become a better place. The hero (Jesus) would win. What we actually see is more or less the opposite of all this, with the final straw being that the hero (Jesus) is in fact crucified as a criminal.

The Bible we might design would be user-friendly. It would contain unambiguous answers to all the world's questions, including the ones we haven't yet asked. Stories would be clearly identified as such, as would factual reports, and placed in different sections (as in a magazine). There would be a clear progression from the beginning to the end, with some kind of summary as to what we have to believe, and what we might expect and when. As we have seen, and will see, the Bible is nothing like that, though some treat it as if it were.

Is it possible then to describe the Bible at all or can we only say what it is not? We began by saying that the Bible is the story of God up to a particular significant point in history, as told by those who believed that they had had an authentic glimpse of the presence of God, and who were able to persuade the later community of faith that that was so. It is the product of communities of faith who are just that: communities of *faith*. That is, their religion derives from a trust in and sense of relationship with God. These communities have always found God puzzling, have always accepted that there is more to know, have always been fascinated by the way God works in the world, and have often been struck as much by God's perceived absence as his presence. It is hardly surprising that the documents produced seem a little piecemeal, unedited, and contradictory. Perhaps it would be helpful to think of them as a series of diaries in which one day everything seems clear, and the next it's all thrown back into confusion. But it is that very unpredictability that, from the perspective of trusting faith, a Christian might say, gives reading the Bible its excitement, its vigour, its relevance and its sheer authenticity. In other words, that's what makes it worth bothering about.

2

The Bible in Ten Minutes

Responding to disaster

Nowadays we're well used to the kind of tragic or traumatic event that causes people of faith to ask: Where was God in all this? How could God let this happen? How is religious faith possible any more after this? These events can be natural disasters, such as an earthquake or tsunami, they can be associated disasters, such as famines or epidemics like AIDS. They can be acts of terror, such as 9/11, state-sponsored wars like the second Gulf war against Iraq, or acts of great human evil, such as was experienced as a result of the Holocaust or slave trade. They have in common the fundamental questions they raise for people who believe in a loving and creative God. From one point of view, the Bible could be said to result from two such traumatic disasters.

The first took place in the seventh and sixth centuries BCE. Like all the biblical action it took place in the countries at the far eastern end of the Mediterranean, and in this case, especially in the countries we now think of as Israel, the occupied Palestinian Territories, Iraq, Syria and Egypt. What happened at the beginning of the sixth century BCE was basically that one of the strongest political powers in the region conquered one of the smallest. Described like that, it sounds like business as usual in this volatile part of the world, but there was much more to it. The small nation of Israel sat between the superpowers of Assyria, Babylon and Egypt. In the eighth century BCE, Assyria had annexed the whole of the northern part of Israel, and all that was left was the southern area known as Judah, including the area around Jerusalem, which was its capital and centre. During the seventh century, the rulers of Judah tried to read the political situation in a way that would allow them to remain independent, by forming alliances with larger nations, but it all came to nothing when Babylon captured and largely destroyed Jerusalem in two waves of attacks in 597 and 587. Each time, the conquerors took away large numbers of the inhabitants of Judah to work as slaves in exile in Babylon. So began the period known as the Exile, which lasted about 50 years: two or three generations.

For the people of Israel this was the kind of disaster that raised huge religious questions. As a people they held a religious belief in a God called Yahweh with whom they believed they enjoyed a special relationship. This God spoke to them in a powerful contemporary way through people called prophets, but the beliefs of this people belonged to a series of stories from more ancient times about how their God had effectively formed the nation after rescuing its ancestors from slavery in Egypt and bringing them to a new land that came to be called Israel. They believed that Yahweh had promised them a land of their own, the land of Israel, that he had promised them lots of descendants to enable them to continue to be a people, a nation, and that he had promised to have a special relationship with them for ever. Everything they knew and believed about God was based on this understanding.

Crisis

If that were a summary of what these people believed about God, then the events of 597 and 587 threw their world into crisis. If God had promised them a land, why were they being forcibly removed from it? If God had promised that they would always be a nation, why were they being taken into exile, with the real possibility that their sense of nationhood would disappear over time? What kind of special relationship would allow the suffering and misery of forced exile? And so there was a crisis about God. Like all such crises there are two possible responses. One is to give up on the idea of God altogether, and to say, in effect, 'We thought that religion had something going for it but we were wrong. There's no point in it all, and probably no such thing as God. It's all a sham.' The other response is to say, 'In the light of this experience, what we thought we knew about God was wrong. Clearly there are new things to be learned, and in this new context we must try and learn them.' That is the response of those who do not want to give up on religion and who want to maintain faith, but who realize that it has to be radically reassessed. The Old Testament comes to us from this second group. It is essentially a record of their quest for meaning.

So what does it consist of? As you might expect from experience nowadays, the most immediate questions in response to a trauma that raises fundamental religious questions are: How can God let this happen? How could God do this to us? How and why has this happened? In the context of the Old Testament, the response to the questions took the form of revisiting the story of the nation, and looking at that for clues as to what could have gone wrong, or what could have been misunderstood about God. The people who were responsible for re-telling that story from all the ancient traditions had their own ideas about what had gone wrong, and told the story from that point of view. Those traditions were supplemented by the more recent 'sightings' of God that were provided by the words of the prophets, whom religious people supposed to have spoken the word of God in specific situations.

All in all, the combination of that story, together with the recent prophetic commentary, makes for quite depressing reading. It tells the tale of a God who had high hopes for making a special relationship with the people of Israel, but then how the whole project was jeopardized time and time again, and eventually, apparently, abandoned, as a result of the refusal of the people to keep their side of the bargain and to maintain a society based on principles of justice, peace, relationship, and truth. And more than that, it wasn't just the people who were at fault, it was their political leaders, people in whom great hopes had been vested but who had not taken their responsibilities seriously. The description of this, in some detail, takes up a fair proportion of the Old Testament. It includes portions of the first five books, especially Deuteronomy, the books through from Joshua to 2 Kings, and the books of the prophets who were writing in the eighth and seventh centuries. This acts both as an answer to the immediate questions but also as a warning for the future. As politicians often say when confronted with the results of an official enquiry into some issue: 'Lessons have been learned. This must not happen again.'

Looking forward: the new religious quest

But it isn't all doom and gloom. Once the people accepted that they were exiles in a foreign land, and had got over the initial stages of coping with their confusion and anger, they began to look forward. Again, they were supported by prophets, who spoke a more hopeful word of God. It described how the people of Israel could have another chance to settle their land and start over again. This led to another re-telling of the story of the nation. This time, a different set of authors were looking for a different set of clues. They didn't so much want to know why it had happened. They wanted to get the positive evidence together for how a return to their land, and the building of a new society there, could be most successful. These authors, too, had a fairly clear idea about what was going to be needed, and they told their story, and adapted the old one, in a way that favoured their view. Their writings are also to be found in portions of the first five books, especially Leviticus; then in the books of Chronicles, Ezra and Nehemiah, together with prophets writing in the sixth century and later.

Then there was the question: What have we learned from all this? We have some views on where we went wrong. We have some views on how we might succeed given another chance, but

The importance of the Old Testament

There are three things that are important to bear in mind, as we think of the Old Testament in this general way. The first is, that although this is all set out as the history of a country called Israel at a specific time in long-ago history, the issues with which it deals are not specific to that situation. They are universal. They are issues faced by anyone who wants to know how best to live their life and how best to organize society. They are issues familiar to anyone who has faced fundamental trauma or personal tragedy. They are contemporary issues to all who today feel a sense of exile, or who feel at odds with the world, who carry a burden of guilt or who are curious about the destiny of the earth and its inhabitants. And within all that, there is a wealth of possible contemporary reference which this book will seek to help uncover.

The second thing to bear in mind is that as the 'Old Testament', this collection does not fully resolve the issues that it raises. It raises questions. It articulates hopes and expectations. It gives us several chapters in a history of God. But it is not the whole story. For Christians the New Testament answers some of the questions more fully, fulfils the promises of the Old Testament and gives us the last word possible about God. Of course, there is always more to say, because if we knew absolutely everything about God he wouldn't be God, but given that, Christians believe Christ to be God's last word on the subject of what God is like.

And the third thing is that the Old Testament provides a vocabulary and idiom in which to talk about these things, which if we were starting from scratch we should probably not use now: words like redemption, messiah, atonement, heaven and resurrection. The Old Testament writers were limited by the language, Hebrew, which they spoke, and limited in the pictures they could draw upon for illustration simile and metaphor by their own relatively narrow experience as a fairly enclosed set of people from a remote spot a long way from here, two or three thousand years before the internet. In order to uncover the universal significance and in order to see how the New Testament relates to the Old, it is to be expected, then, that we shall have to do a fair bit of translating from those times in order to understand what some of those words and pictures might mean today. That is perfectly legitimate, though that kind of work can be a bit subjective and not everyone will always agree. That is one of the issues between those who think that taking the Bible seriously means accepting its literal truth, and those who think that to take it seriously you must do the translating and detective work to see what its truth might be for today.

Another crisis

So much for the first trauma: the Exile, which gave birth to the Old Testament as we know it. What was the second trauma? The answer is: the crucifixion of Jesus. Everyone might accept that this was a tragedy and perhaps even, an injustice, but why was it a religious trauma like the Exile, the Holocaust or 9/11? The answer is that for those who believed that Jesus was God, crucifixion threw that belief into doubt, because everything that people thought they knew about God up to that point demanded that Gods do not suffer and do not get crucified as criminals. If your view of God is that he is both loving and powerful, then the crucifixion means either that he is not powerful enough to be able stop it, or he is not loving enough to want to do so. Religious Jews, passing the site of the crucifixion are recorded in the Bible as saying: 'Let him come down from the cross and we will believe in him. He saved others. Let him save himself.' This is not just callous talk. It is an eminently reasonable thing to say to someone you must inevitably consider to be an imposter because he is being crucified.

So once again religious folk are faced with a choice: either abandon any belief that Jesus is a special revelation of God, and perhaps in the process abandon religious belief altogether, or take the view that this new chapter in the story of God means that we've got it a bit wrong so far, and that there is actually more to learn about God than we had imagined. That means, in turn, that we have to come to terms with the idea of a God who can suffer and die, a God who can take the initiative to relinquish strength for weakness, and the idea of a religious community that does not exist simply to make sure it's doing the things that it imagines God wants in order to persuade him to keep the world safe and vindicate his people. For those who want to maintain faith, this involves a huge re-writing of what we mean by God, or by a religious life, what we mean by a religious community, even what we mean by worship. The New Testament is the record of those who attempted that task. It also means looking back over the tradition up to that point and reassessing it. The first Christians did not believe that the Old Testament had got it completely wrong, but they did believe that, as we saw within the Old Testament itself, some reinterpretation was necessary to make the whole story coherent in the light of this latest revelation. And so words and images from the Old Testament are frequently referred to, usually in the context of their reinterpretation, in the New.

The first Easter and all that

The key event that gave birth to the New Testament is what we might call the first Easter, and all that involves. Scholars reckon that that probably took place around 29 CE. Thereafter we have to imagine the first Christian communities being born and beginning the task of reinterpreting what religious faith means now. It's another 20 years or so before we have any record of written work from these groups and then what we get is a series of letters. Fortunately, these early Christians wanted to talk with each other. By the time the letters are being written, Christianity has won converts all over the eastern Mediterranean, as well as in the areas of Jerusalem and the Galilee where most of Jesus' ministry seems to have taken place. Some of those letters now form part of the New Testament, and that is a fascinating thought in itself. No other religion has a series of letters as part of its holy writings – especially letters that are as ordinary as these, dealing with inconsequential bits of personal news, as well as with issues that have arisen in these new Christian communities. The letters continue to be written and some of them are collected and kept. Those that are part of our Bible are perhaps only a proportion of the letters written. Many were written by Paul, but others were written by other Christian leaders. The earliest we might date around 49 CE and the latest could be as late as the second century.

History and argument

One of the ways in which we can relate these letters to each other and get some sort of handle on how to interpret them, is by comparing them with the account in the book called The Acts of the Apostles, or Acts for short. This purports to be a history of the early Church up to about the year 62, and in particular tells the story of two early Christian leaders, Peter and Paul. We have to approach it with a little caution. No history is written without some kind of agenda, and the author of Acts wants his readers to believe that Christianity is here to stay in a big way, and is moving onward and upward at a rate – proof of its divine inspiration. He also wants to commend it as a good thing and something that political powers need not be suspicious of. That means that the story might be skewed or that sources might have been chosen carefully. Also we have to be aware that the author is probably Luke, and that this is part two of a major work whose first part is the Gospel of Luke. But if we accept that, Acts is about as good a place as any to start to read the New Testament. Here we learn about the tensions of moving from an understanding of religion that is national, and whose adherents speak one language and accept one history and culture, to an understanding that is international. Within the early Christian communities there are many local cultures and histories, and some of the terms that can be used to describe the significance of Jesus successfully to Jews would mean nothing at all to those from Rome, Greece or Egypt. Acts describes this growing process of internationalism, with the changes that it brings. There are new names to try out for this community. There are new forms of ministry not tried before. There are new images and pictures available to describe Jesus and the Church. They key term is 'new'. Acts describes with real enthusiasm the newness and difference that Christianity brings. It is a breath of fresh air to the religious world.

The earliest batch of letters captures this sense of adventure and newness. They are written by the convert Paul to places like Thessalonica and Corinth, places where Paul and his companions have, according to Acts, made missionary journeys to bring Christianity to new areas. These letters respond to the questions raised in these places. They share good practice and new ideas. They encourage and build up fellowship and become a means of showing pastoral support and care from a distance. For today's readers they give a valuable insight into the adventure of doing theology. We see communities grappling with inherited traditions and trying to interpret them in the light of their recent experience and of the new things they have just learned about God, in a way that makes a difference in their situations. This is how 'Christianity' as such develops into something more formulated and organized. A second later batch of letters reflects this rather more organized stage of affairs. There is then a third stage with letters that show how hard it is to maintain any kind of control over what people describe as 'Christian'. There has never been copyright on the word 'Christian' and unfortunately, nowadays more than ever perhaps, the most bizarre manifestations of religion can be described by some as 'Christian' even though most Christians would not want to be associated with them. In the later letters of the New Testament we see attempts to put boundaries around what can properly be described as Christian, attempts to define what is meant by various kinds of ministry, and attempts to claim that certain beliefs and practices are orthodox and some are heresy. These later letters appear to have lost the vitality and pioneering sense of openness to possibility that characterized the earlier ones, but they do give an insight into how religious communities develop.

Church FAQs

Just as the Old Testament describes particular situations that have a much wider application, so these accounts of the growth of a Church provide interesting reading for those who are members of churches today. They describe both pitfalls and possibilities, which are readily recognizable to today's Christians. They contain, if you like, universal Frequently Asked Questions for church members. They do show a number of things that are innovative and new. They show how theology is done, by relating the old stories and what we know about God to specific contexts and allowing a creative conversation to take place between them. Nowadays we would call this process theological reflection, and there will be opportunity for it throughout this book. They show an understanding of the Church that is more like a coalition of groups with important things in common than an organization that can sign up to a common declaration. They show a willingness to experiment with mission and ministry, and a desire to explore the possibility of freedom from traditional ideas of religion. However, what they do not contain is any account of the life and ministry of Jesus – the main reason for their existence is somehow taken for granted. It may be that these stories were handed on perfectly adequately by word of mouth in a kind of oral tradition and in local versions. But there came a point where that was no longer good enough.

The news

The stories and reflections about Jesus that go to make up the four Gospels were circulating for a long time in oral form before they were written down. The first Gospel (literally 'Good News') was probably not published until the early 60s, more than 30 years after the events it describes, and that is a long time in anyone's estimation. That first Gospel was probably the one we call Mark. Two other writers got hold of Mark and together with other material, some of which they shared, they wrote two other Gospels, Matthew and Luke. Why they did so is not clear, but they evidently did not find that Mark answered the questions that were being asked in their communities. The Gospel of John is very different from the other three, but the underlying story it tells is a similar one, of a controversial ministry including healing and other so-called 'signs', demonstrating that this is in fact a new and final revelation from God, followed by a detailed account of the betrayal, trial and crucifixion of Jesus and its aftermath. Some scholars believe that before the whole Gospels were published, the account of Jesus' last week, the so-called 'Passion Narrative' (that is, the story of his suffering) circulated separately, and that observation leads to something that it is important to note about Gospels.

Gospels are not biographies of Jesus. Biographies usually contain lots of information about the biographer and these do not. For the same reason it is wrong to think of them as random memoirs of the apostles. But apart from that they are very selective in the material they present. Assuming that Jesus was born in 4 BCE (I know, but just trust me), the Gospels deal almost exclusively with just three years of his life, and for the most part with just one week – the week leading up to his crucifixion. Deeper study shows them to be sophisticated and cleverly crafted works that are seeking to address questions being asked in the early church communities, and particularly that most controversial of questions, Why did Jesus have to suffer and die? To that extent, the Gospels actually look more like Passion Narratives (see above) with an introduction. Of course, other questions were being asked. What was the relationship between Jesus' baptism and the baptism of believers? What form of worship was appropriate for Christians? How should they pray? At what point did Jesus become God – was it at his baptism (was he somehow adopted) or was he God from the start? The birth and infancy stories that are an attempt to answer this question are actually among the latest to be added to the Gospels even though they appear first, and of course only two of the four Gospels have them anyway.

Continuing questions

So the New Testament consists of letters and Gospels. The letters were written first but logically, I suppose, it makes sense to put the story of Jesus first, though it would be interesting to see a Bible that had the order Acts – letters – Gospels, which is how we might read it with most understanding. There is one more book in the New Testament that we have not mentioned. That is the last book, the Revelation to John. This book is an example of a particularly Jewish form of writing, which flourished for around 250 years around the time of the birth of Christ. From the Greek word for revelation, this way of writing is called 'apocalyptic'. The New Testament book of Revelation was probably written in the final years of the first century and, rather like the Wisdom writing in the Old Testament, it is a means of reflecting on some of the implications of faith from the standpoint of the political realities of the world. In fact it revisits some of those universal questions with which the Bible began, about whether goodness really can overcome evil, and whether love will prove stronger than hatred, and essentially whether God's will for the world will prevail in the light of the enormous power of earthly systems and organizations, such as the Roman Empire. It leaves us with questions that are contemporary for us too, like: How is it possible to continue to proclaim good news about a God who has set people free and rescued people from exploitation, when the evidence of our own experience contradicts that with every news bulletin?

The New Testament gives us hints as to how the story continues. It speaks of a Holy Spirit that will be God's ongoing presence in the Church. It speaks of hopes for the future, and a new estimate of the destiny of creation. In Revelation, it assures us that the war is won even though there might be some battles yet to fight.

There is no denying that the Bible is an unusual volume, but it need not be daunting. It will be useful to keep the outline of this chapter in mind as we work through the individual parts of the Bible. But before we do that and get engrossed in the detail, there is one more part of the big picture we need to address: What is the Bible about?

3

What is the Bible About?

As I begin to write this chapter on my PC, I half expect to see a notice appear: 'you have performed an illegal operation and the program will be shut down', because this chapter will attempt to set out a summary of some of the main themes of the Bible, and actually the Bible is not intended to be read like that. It is not organized as a systematic treatise or divided into neat subject areas; and to describe its themes in just a few paragraphs might suggest that it is. We are doing something, in other words, that goes against the grain of the Bible. Nevertheless, bearing that very much in mind, I hope that this brief sketch might help readers to recognize some of the Bible's main areas of interest, but also to remember that these are played and replayed over centuries, and that they change, develop and react as each generation of communities of faith reflects upon them in their own situation. It might help maintain that reflective character of the Bible if we think of a series of headings, that say not 'What the Bible thinks about such-and-such', but rather, 'Making sense of . . .'. And most basically of all, the Bible wants to *make sense of God*. That is *whom* it is about.

Making sense of God

A record of people's experience of God over centuries is bound to be varied. The New Testament provides us with accounts of Jesus, whom Christians believe to be a complete revelation of God. After the first Easter, the continuing presence and activity of God is described in terms of the work of the Holy Spirit. The Spirit of God is also referred to in the Old Testament to describe God's activity. The words breath, wind and spirit translate the same word in Hebrew, and there are many instances of those terms being used to express the dynamic quality of God. In the Old Testament, God is largely known by what God does, but people of faith reflected on that and ascribed different titles to God, many of them by analogy, drawn from their everyday lives. One writer has found the following titles in the prophetic writings, for example: God is father, brother, mother, husband, friend, warrior, shepherd, farmer, metal-worker, builder, potter, fuller, physician, judge, water-seller, king and scribe. That collection in turn gives us a more rounded picture of how people understood God's activity, his relationship with his people, and his character.

It is commonly believed that Old Testament people experienced God first as a *liberator*. As we shall see in the next chapter, the story of the people of Israel really begins with an account of *bringing people from slavery* in Egypt to a land of their own. The earliest creeds or confessions of faith that we read in the Old Testament tell this story. It's true that individuals like Abraham, Jacob, and Isaac are described as having a relationship with God before the slavery, but the relationship between God and the people as a whole is described as beginning there. Having freed people from slavery, the way the story progresses, God's next task is *to free them from chaos* by providing them with an infrastructure of civilization through the law, and through the appointment of kings. As we have seen, some of those kings were not up to the job and, in any case, there was a view that putting power in the hands of a king was wrong in principle anyway and bound to fail. And indeed, God's new state did fail. First, it split into two parts, at odds with each other. Then the northern part, Israel, was conquered by Assyria. Later the southern part, Judah, was conquered by Babylon, leading to the Exile. The recriminations then led to a greater awareness of the distance between, on the one hand, what God wanted and, on the other, what people did. The term 'sin' is sometimes used to describe this distance and its symptoms – breakdown of communications, anger, corruption, violence, infidelity, unwillingness to observe proper boundaries in human behaviour (an example of which would be incest), abuse of power, to name a few more obvious ones. God's final work of liberation is to *free people from sin*. Whereas freedom from slavery and chaos involves the political and civil process, showing God working in the world, freedom from sin has both a corporate and a personal aspect. As the Bible progresses into the New Testament, we see more evidence of the individual interpretation of sin, as personal wrongdoing, and less of the communal, though there are some striking examples of the latter as, for example, in the story about the sheep and the goats, a story about ultimate judgement, in Matthew chapter 25.

As we see the movement from political liberation to freeing individuals from their sin, the vocabulary changes. In connection with sin, we are more likely to think of God as a saviour than a liberator, though the intention is the same. The antidote to sin is forgiveness, and we see that having a more personal aspect as well, in the New Testament, though the corporate is not entirely absent, as, for example, in Jesus' cry from the cross, 'Forgive them father for they do not know what they are doing.' Forgiving and saving are closely related to healing, reconciling and re-integrating into community and being brought to wholeness or at-one-ment. The language of the slave market gives an insight into the early psychology that sees people who do wrong as being slaves to sin. God's role is to buy them back from that evil master, or to redeem them. Early Christians saw the death of Jesus as being connected with this process in some way.

It was probably as a result of the Exile that Old Testament people came to believe that there was only one God and that he was therefore God of all creation and God of all history. Belief in God as a creator is a late, rather than an early, way of understanding him. This belief allows more sophisticated thinking about God's purpose for the world and its peoples, and about its final destiny. Dissatisfaction with aspects of the experienced world (Why does there have to be hunger, disease, danger and sadness, for example?) led to prophetic imagining of how creation could be improved and how God might bring that about.

Making sense of communities

All other kinds of 'making sense' are related to making sense of God. Another important area of interest is *making sense of the human community and of the Church*. According to the Bible, God calls the human community into being: it is his initiative. He has a particular relationship, first with the whole created order, then more particularly with the people of Israel, and finally with the whole of humankind again. We might think of the relationship with Israel as a model of the kind of relationship God wants to have with the whole of humankind. The Old Testament speaks of an agreement or Covenant (indeed the word 'testament' means just that) between God and his people. So the New Testament is an updating of the agreement that takes account of Jesus. The agreement describes God's character as one of faithfulness, loving kindness, truthfulness and mercy. God is experienced as being interested and involved in the life of his people. In turn, they promise to organize society along lines that will promote righteousness, justice, peace and harmonious relationships.

It is important to realize that the Bible never simply gives a list of rules for human behaviour, as if it were a diktat from on high. People are urged to behave in a particular way and organize society in a particular way for a reason. The overriding reason is usually to imitate God, but this is often spelt out in terms of specifics. In the Old Testament, for example, people are told that they should be generous and hospitable to strangers and foreigners. Almost invariably they are reminded then that once they were strangers, and in need of hospitality and generosity themselves. In the New Testament, Paul takes a great interest in the grace of God: that is God's action in coming down to the human level and making friends with us anew. Paul sees here a model of the strong becoming weak, voluntarily, in order to further the relationship, which he commends to Christians he writes to. Often, in his letters, he sets out a description of what God has done which is 'graceful', and then urges Christians to be graceful in their turn. As God has been a reconciler, so humans have a vocation or ministry of reconciliation themselves. Always the initiative is God's. We love him because he first loved us.

One important emphasis that the Bible places is actually on community. This is not a religious volume that describes individual as opposed to communal life; something meant to be accessed by individuals about individuals. The model of God taking a special interest in Israel as a community is taken up by New Testament writers, and applied to the infant Church. They would like to see the Church as the kind of community God wants. And so, as we see its life, ministry, and liturgy develop we see initiatives designed to promote the idea of a connected community with each member both contributing and benefiting. We see a special regard for the powerless, the outsider, the disadvantaged and the poor. Community life is designed to help them, but also to help the rich and powerful become more truly human in the process. In the New Testament, as in the Old, liturgy is a communal affair and, apart from giving voice to expressions of thankfulness and praise, it gives opportunity for joint confession, joint commitment and joint acceptance of a view of life that values sharing, sacrifice and selflessness. The New Testament picture of the Church that brings those things to mind most readily is, perhaps, one used (and probably invented) by Paul: the Body of Christ. There are over 90 other pictures, but all describe something with a corporate character.

The New Testament has much less to say about the nation or about civic society than does the Old, for obvious reasons. The Old Testament gives us a record of a relatively powerful nation that is able to make decisions about its political life. Politics and secular life are of great interest, and regarded as part of the religious agenda. In the New Testament, Christians are relatively powerless politically. There is little interest in secular politics, which are presented as being of much less interest to God, though they are mentioned from time to time, and especially in the writings of Luke. However, the letters in the New Testament do have much to say about citizenship and about the relationship between church and state. But the key interest is in the Church, and questions around: what it is; what is new about it in comparison with other forms of religious life, and how it should develop. In the Gospels there is a different emphasis.

The gospel message: making sense of Jesus

Jesus' message, in the first three Gospels at least, is all about the kingdom of God. This is a way of describing a new society, in which the flaws of ordinary life as we know it are removed, and in which God's rule is transparently upheld. This message is related to the ministry of John the Baptist, who is urging people to get ready for this kingdom. Jesus' main teaching is in the form of short stories called parables, all of which are about the kingdom of God, or the kingdom of heaven (they are the same thing). They attempt to get people interested in it and committed to it. The language about 'kingdoms' comes from the Old Testament and is a good example of how the New Testament has to work with the ideas and vocabulary of those particular times and those particular people. We might not use that language nowadays but we could all compile a list of the things that are so wrong with our society that we despair of human agency to change them. Only something more cataclysmic can bring about the new age we long for. The Bible has a particular interest in these changes and how they might be brought about. They are changes that are necessary not only in the hearts of individuals though. Human society, and indeed the whole created order, need to be renewed as well.

Of course, the New Testament has a special interest in *making sense of Jesus*. The writings came from a deep sense of certainty that Jesus was God, but as the story unfolds, that creates more problems than it solves. The issue of why Jesus had to suffer and die if he was really God, is one that the early

Gospels have to cope with. Indeed, initially, that question may have prompted at least one of them to be written. Then, we observe how the writers 'package' Jesus so that their readers can understand his significance. Who is he really? Old Testament readers have been led to expect some startling new initiative from God to establish the new age, and the new kingdom. This means there will be a new king. The tradition in Israel was that kings were anointed with oil, and the Hebrew word for some-one who had been anointed like that was 'messiah'. When that word was translated into Greek, the language of the New Testament, it reads as 'christos'. Those two words give us not only two different 'titles' for Jesus but also a way of under-standing his significance that relates him to the expectations and religious beliefs of the people of those times, from a Jewish culture. Other similar terms were 'Son of God' and 'Son of Man'.

Sometimes we see in the New Testament, descriptions of people who are confused about who Jesus is. 'Are you the one who is to come,' they say, 'or shall we look for another?' They continually ask for a sign. Is Jesus a second Moses, or a second Elijah or a second David? The Gospels attempt to help us. Such descriptions only really ring a bell, of course, with people from a Jewish background. When Christianity began to move into the wider world, new ways of describing his significance had to be found, and new titles attached to him, as he was 're-packaged'. Greek-speaking Jews living in foreign countries had developed their own religious vocabulary and understanding, and titles such as 'Lord' or the 'Word of God' (as we see in the first chapter of John's Gospel) spoke to them more directly. And as people who had no knowledge of Jewish traditions at all became Christians, ways of describing his importance based on language and ideas from mystery religions, civic religion, and other understandings began to take their place. These are all ways of understanding Jesus' significance that relate to the culture and vocabulary of long ago. The question all Christians want answered is: Who is Jesus for me now? Modern Christians have generally adopted the words we find in the New Testament, without always understanding their history or their implications. There are too, as we shall see, attempts to find new ways, new pictures to describe Jesus, for which the New Testament acts both as a model and an encouragement.

Who Jesus is is related closely to the question: What did Jesus do? The Gospels approach this question by telling us about his ministry and his death. They use another religious term, current at the time, to show that his death is related to *the resurrection*, that is, the sure sign of the beginning of the new age, which people sought. The letters in the New Testament make no mention at all of the details of the ministry of Jesus. The important thing for Paul, who wrote most of them, is that God has taken an initiative. Most religions work on the basis that the task of human beings is to try and persuade their god to keep the world safe and to keep them well, by doing the right thing, offering the right sacrifices and attending the right ceremonies. Essentially, the ball is in the human court. Such help as religions like that give, is in the form of rules and regulations and laws that people can keep, in order to appease their god appropriately and finally be vindicated. For Paul, that is the exact opposite of what God's initiative in Jesus has demonstrated, and the exact opposite of what Christianity is about. For him, Christianity means that there is nothing that we can do to achieve our own salvation. Only the grace of God can do that. And so the kind of religion that is based on rules, regulations and laws is superseded and defunct. Jesus, as the risen Lord, is proof of this for Paul, and that is such an exciting idea that he spends most of his letters working out its implications.

Making sense of us

Making sense of ourselves is an important reason why Christians read the Bible. In it we find many examples of people trying to cope with problems that we recognize from our own experience. One of those is about human nature. Why is it so difficult to do the right thing? Why is the wrong thing so much more attractive? As we have seen, the language of 'sin' is used freely to describe these negative aspects, not just of individual life and conduct, but also of the problems of the wider community and world. One of the basic questions the Bible addresses is a very modern one: What's going to happen in the end? Will good win out over evil, and will God's good purposes defeat all that the powers of evil can throw up? Or, will God's plans for good always and inevitably be thwarted by human corruption? The Bible issues a resounding 'yes' to the first proposition. God and goodness will, and indeed, have won. And that winning is tied up in the minds of the writers with Jesus' death on the cross. In a profound way, this is seen as the defeat of evil. His death on the cross was 'for our sins'. The problem is that ordinary experience does not bear out that confidence. For most people at most times in history it has not actually looked as if good were winning out over evil. The opposite has seemed more likely. Writers have to encourage some congregations to believe in the 'victory of the cross', in that sense. The Bible tells us that we are important, that we matter and that we are loved. It tells us that sin does have an antidote – forgiveness – and that we stand forgiven. It tells us that we have second chances and that no human situation is beyond redemption. It urges us to be creative and to echo God's relationship with us, to others. But the way it assures us of this is varied and multi-layered. The arguments of Paul state it in one way, but the stories of Old Testament characters, and Jesus' own stories, describe our flawed condition, and give us hope, in equal measure.

Making sense of creation

The claims that the Bible makes for Jesus are such that his activity is presented to us as a key moment in the history of the world of meaning. But what is that world's relation to the physical world? From the time of the Exile onwards, as the people of Israel grew in their conviction that there was just one God, it was clear to them that he must be the *God of all creation* and the

God of all history. Making sense of those claims is an area of biblical interpretation that is most open to abuse and which causes great controversy. There are those who want to say that God created the world in seven days, and who therefore put religion at odds with science. There are also those who think that believing in a God of all history means that Christians should not be interested in the here and now of this life, but should be much more aware of the impending end of the world, and the coming Armageddon. The difficulty in unravelling exactly what we might believe in these areas is not helped by the fact that all Bible writings come from a pre-scientific age, and they betray an understanding of the physical world that now-adays, at best, we would call primitive.

The thought that God is a God of all creation was an exciting one in the Old Testament.

- If God is the God of all creation, then we ought to be able to learn something about him from observing what he has created.
- By looking at the patterns of nature, or perhaps more particularly, by observing how human relations operate, we might learn more about what God intended, and so, more about God himself. The book of Proverbs in the Old Testament is full of those kinds of observation about how the world works. By looking at the design, we can learn more about the designer.
- Declaring that God is creator is a way of saying that no one else is the world's creator, and that if God is creator, that gives us clues as to the kind of world it is, and is meant to be.
- For Christians, the writings about creation give us a reason to study the physical world and to be interested in science and the scientific enterprise.
- To describe God as a creator is to say something about the nature of God. He is not a destroyer, but is interested in creation, in working involvement, and that means there is a very real point of contact between humankind and God. We also are called to work and create.

- In any reflection about God as creator, there is something to do with the power and authority of God. That is certainly the line taken in chapters 40–55 of the prophet Isaiah – one of the chief places in the Bible where God is described as creator.
- To consider God as responsible for creating the world gives us a mechanism for thanksgiving for all that the world contains, of the kind that we see in harvest festivals in our own, and ancient, cultures.
- This doctrine gives us a religious reason for being good stewards of the earth's resources.
- It also gives us a way of understanding the relation between different bits of creation. This is another contemporary theme, as in the debate about whether animals have rights, for example.

Making sense of vocation

The New Testament does not contain this kind of writing and reflection about creation. It does, however, have an interest in the possibilities that God has created for human life and activity. We might call this area, *vocation*, that is, literally, what we are called to be and do. Paul has much to say about this. The concept of vocation begins with the belief that everything in the world, all that we have and enjoy, including our own personal attributes, all these things are gifts from God. Whatever we achieve is not because we deserve it, or have earned it, or have won it, or because we're morally better than others. Everything we achieve is evidence of God's gifts to us, part of his 'grace'. As with the other gifts of creation we are expected to use our gifts responsibly and with proper acknowledgement of their source. That in turn will lead us to see other people differently, with a new kind of respect, and perhaps a new kind of interest.

Thinking about God as a God of all history helped Old Testament people to put some kind of framework around their lives. Writings on this subject are among the latest in the Old Testament.

- This too has something to say about the power and authority of God. However, the more the Bible portrays God as powerful and authoritative in this way, the more distant he becomes. Something of the close and immediate relationship is lost, and God is understood more through world events and through a host of intermediaries.
- The plus side is that Old Testament people were assured that life had a purpose, events had a meaning, and the world had a destiny.
- One particular way of writing called 'apocalyptic' deals with this subject and we shall cover it in more detail in due course, but an important role of this writing is to make sense of the gap between experience and faith, and especially to make sense of suffering. Suffering could be seen as 'for a purpose', and vindication for those who were suffering or oppressed could be seen as coming 'in the next stage of history', the 'age to come'.

In the New Testament, Christians tended to see Jesus himself as a significant person in God's plan for the world, and his incarnation (that is, his time as a human being) as a significant moment in the world's history. Much of what the Old Testament had looked for was believed by Christians to have been fulfilled in Jesus, but the deficit between faith and experience still had to be addressed. In time this gave rise to a belief in the return of Jesus at some future point, though there is much debate about whether Jesus himself meant to give support to that view.

Making sense of suffering

Making sense of suffering and evil is one of the most profound subjects that humans reflect upon. The presence of evil and the experience of suffering is a problem for everyone, but has a special significance for those who believe that God has in some way designed creation and history. Why allow suffering in the design? Particularly, why allow innocents to suffer? And where did evil come from? The Bible gives us a range of reflections on these issues.

- The simplest response is to say that suffering is connected with behaviour, and so with sin. People who sin are punished and people who do right are rewarded. We might think of this as a primitive view, but it is held by very many people nowadays who, when tragedy strikes a good person say things like 'What did they do to deserve this?' In the New Testament we see the view held by people who want to explain illness in this way, and who aren't quite sure whether people need healing or forgiveness. Some notable episodes in Jesus' ministry involve controversy about this.
- Early attempts to deal with sin involved a ritual in which all the community's sins were ceremonially placed on an animal, which was then sent out to wander in the wilderness – the so-called scapegoat. That too, we might consider primitive, but evidently it is still a way that is used to deal with society's ills.
- The innovative new idea of God's forgiveness was a way of coping with sin, but what was needed was a separation of sin and suffering because the problem with that view is that it is at odds with our experience. We all know good people who suffer, and many of us know bad people who don't.
- Late Old Testament writings give us explanations we have already mentioned, for example, that suffering in this world will be compensated for in the next, and that in any case, it's all for a purpose.
- A more profound reflection in this direction sees suffering as achieving something. It can be 'redemptive'. This is a more attractive view that is closer to the experience of some. Most of us in retrospect at least can point to an experience which was unpleasant at the time but which has helped to make us the people we are, or which achieved something worthwhile. However, some suffering seems pointless, even in retrospect, and the attempt to find some reason for it all is pastorally dangerous.

- The most profound reflection on suffering in the Old Testament comes from the book of Job. This is a kind of novel about a good man who suffers unjustly. Most of the book is concerned to show how inadequate are the current explanations of this state of affairs, such as we are considering here, but at one point Job actually meets God in his suffering. This opens the way to new patterns of thinking about God.
- In the New Testament, suffering is a major theme. The main thing that fundamentally separates Christianity from other religions is that it was born out of the suffering of God. In trying to make sense of this, writers develop the Old Testament idea that suffering can achieve something and can be redemptive, and so some of them make the connection between the cross and salvation.
- Writers like Paul also take a different perspective. They conclude that Jesus' suffering and death tells us something new about God, and that we should not think about him as a figure who controls the world, but as one who can suffer and be weak. So there is an emerging view that God shares suffering rather than causes it, and that it is part of the role of the Church to share suffering as well.

If you find this summary of the Bible's main contents all a bit condensed and difficult, don't worry because we shall be returning to all these themes as we begin to look at the text itself. However, hopefully it will have been useful to have some kind of overview of the concerns of the Bible. For those who aren't sure, this is what religion's all about. On the one hand, it's about the human condition. On the other, it's about our understanding of who God is and what he does, based on the experience of people over thousands of years. The Bible is the record of those who want to maintain that religious faith is important, and that it should be worked with and then handed on.

The remainder of the book will suggest how we can 'get started' on various parts of the biblical text. For ease of reference we shall work through the Bible from Genesis to Revelation.

In each short chapter we shall attempt to answer these three important questions:

• What does this portion of the Bible contain?
• What do we need to know in order to make sense of it?
• How can we use it and relate it to our own experience?

Part Two

Getting Started with the Bible

4

Getting Started on
Genesis and Exodus

What's included?

On the face of it, **Genesis** and **Exodus** are easy, straightforward books to access and read.

Genesis

Genesis 1—11, which forms a kind of separate or discrete section of the book, contains a series of stand-alone stories that are dramatic and memorable. This is the kind of material likely to be found in any book of Bible stories, and they form part of our folklore. These include stories about:

- Adam and Eve, 'the first people'.
- Cain and Abel, whose brotherly dispute gives us a first example of violence and contains the memorable phrase, 'Am I my brother's keeper?'
- Noah who survived a great flood by building an ark.
- The tower of Babel, setting out an explanation of why there are so many languages.

It is also in this section that we find descriptions of creation.

From **Genesis 12 to the end** of the book of Genesis, there is a longer continuous story, a kind of family saga. Like all such stories, the plot revolves around interesting and varied people and the relations between them. The characters include all the usual suspects: the black sheep, the scheming mother, the jealous brothers, the wronged woman, and so on. The story begins with a man called Abram who changes his name to Abraham after an encounter with God. That name means, 'father of a people' and the subsequent story shows the development of what will become the nation of Israel. The other main characters in the story are Isaac, Jacob (whose name changes to Israel) and Joseph.

The story is told in a clever yet very simple way that maintains our interest. The bit of the story that deals with Joseph, for example, is so well told that it has formed the basis of a successful Lloyd Webber musical: *Joseph and his Amazing Technicolour Dreamcoat*. The fortunes of Joseph are constantly changing. There's sex interest, violence, humour, mystery, and a happy ending. It's good pantomime stuff.

Exodus

Exodus begins another major story in the Old Testament, and introduces another major character, Moses. This story does not revolve around the *Dallas*-like activities of Jacob's family, though there is a rather unlikely link between that family and the subsequent people of Israel, on whom attention now focuses. They are slaves in Egypt, and the story of Exodus is about their liberation from slavery and their rather tortuous and artificial-sounding journey across the Sinai desert to freedom. This theme of Exodus is deeply ingrained in the consciousness of the Jewish people, and was a key way, for example, in which their location in the present land of Israel, in the middle of the twentieth century, was understood.

Some of the elements of that story are also very well known and part of our folk memory. The account of Moses' birth and the story of 'Moses in the bulrushes', is a standard. The rescue of the people from Egypt is the basis of the Jewish festival of Passover. The climax of the stories about the desert period is the receiving of the so-called 'Ten Commandments' at a holy mountain, and that too has been the subject of a famous twentieth-century film. The whole account is very exciting and is indeed a good story well told.

What these parts of the Bible present to us is, first of all, an introduction to some of the key questions about human experience. One possibility is to read the section Genesis 1—11 as if it presented 'the problem'. If so, the rest of the Bible presents the tortuous route to 'the solution'. This is a way of reading that we find underlying Handel's *Messiah*, for example; and in most Christmastide services of Nine Lessons and Carols. From Genesis 12 onwards we are introduced to the means of coping with 'the problem'. Essentially, it's a story about faith and obedience at odds with sin and disobedience, and so Abraham is presented as a man of faith. It is his family and descendants who are to have a special role in subsequent history, and thus we begin to take an interest in them as they become less like a family and more like a nation. The story of the nation then takes over. We read how essentially it is formed, and through the giving of the law, the basis on which it will operate. This is the story as it's presented, but we need to dig a little deeper to read and hear it with real understanding.

Before we come to that, it is worth noting some key biblical language, themes and ideas that are introduced here. We have already looked at some of the things that are said here about God. Indeed, these portions really introduce God to us. He is creative, loving and interested in the world. He works best with those who work with him, and his aim is freedom, liberation and the fulfilment of potential. He is a God who acts, a God who promises and a God who keeps faith. Other key words and themes include:

- **Election.** This is the term that describes God's choosing this particular people to fulfil his purposes. He is a God who calls and chooses both individuals and nations to have a part in the destiny of the world.
- **Land.** One part of the promise God makes is that his people will inhabit a particular stretch of land. This promise, as the

story tells it, is made by God to Abraham way before the nation is formed, and way before there is any hint of slavery in Egypt. But it begins to be kept as the slaves leave Egypt and make for this land. The land is therefore not just a convenient place to live, but also an important part of God's promise and an important pledge of his faithfulness.

• **Covenant.** This is the word used to describe the overall agreement between God and people. God promises land, descendants and a special relationship to the people of Israel, as they will become. He promises to be a God who is faithful, loving, merciful and really interested in keeping the relationship alive. The people's part in all this begins to be set out towards the end of the book of Exodus in chapters 20—24, which includes God's ten words, popularly known as the ten commandments. In chapter 24 we read of a ceremony to ratify the whole thing.

In effect, most readers then skip on through the books of Leviticus and Numbers. These books seem to contain re-tellings of the journeys in the wilderness, with lots of additions to the covenant obligations, often dealing with all kinds of religious ceremony, which appear to be of little interest to us nowadays. Their style is far less reader-friendly, and the easy story-telling style is virtually absent. Instead there are lists of regulations, lists of names, and descriptions of obscure religious practices. In some ways it's a shame that we are tempted to skip through this, though it is understandable. As we shall see, the book of Leviticus in particular is written from a very interesting standpoint, and can make fascinating reading. But, of course, we prefer stories, and especially stories about people whose problems and experiences strike chords with our own.

What then do we need to know to make sense of this material?

There are probably three key things to bear in mind.

The **first** is that although this looks like one continuous story told by one author, in fact it is a weaving together of more than one story, told by very different people at different times in Israel's history. It might be helpful to think of two main stories joined together (though the entire picture is much more complicated than that, and these two stories draw on lots of different sources, probably from different periods of history). These two stories reached their final form at different times, and in response to different situations. In order to understand the differences, imagine this scenario.

Suppose that two different political parties were going to commission the writing of a history of Britain. One party's political views, let's call it party A, are that what makes Britain great, and indeed what makes it Britain, are its institutions and heritage. That history might concentrate on the development of the monarchy, the institutions of law and government and the achievements of the military. People reading that history might conclude that for Britain to maintain its identity and be great in the future, it should support and uphold those institutions. Party B has a different perspective. They believe that the very institutions championed by party A are dragging Britain down, and that there should be a redistribution of power more generally in the population. The history they wrote would concentrate on the achievements of ordinary people, on the abuses of power by the strong, on the great gains made as a result of universal suffrage, free education and health services open to all. People reading this might reach a very different conclusion about what were needed in the future for Britain to maintain its identity and be great. And more than that, imagine how both those histories might change, depending on when they were written. Histories of Britain written before World War One, for example, would be very different from those written at the beginning of the twenty-first century. And yet, on the face of it, the histories would be dealing with the same story, the same 'facts', sometimes even the same people. The key thing to recognize is that histories that are recounted for a purpose are told in a way that suits and supports that purpose.

The two stories that we come across here and in other parts of the Old Testament are a bit like that. They are written by people who want to know how Israel can best fulfil its destiny. And just as World War One, in the example above, was a key moment, for Bible writers, as we have seen, the Exile was very important. Those who wrote before the Exile, have a very different perspective from those who wrote after. The amazing thing is that these two approaches, though very different, are both included in the Bible. In a sense, we are invited to make up our minds which of them is right. Read in this way, chapters 1— 11 of Genesis could be said, not so much to describe 'the problem', but rather to describe 'the dilemma'.

*For example, look at **Genesis chapter 10**, and then **Genesis 11.1–9**. Genesis 10 describes diversity as a natural consequence of God's command in 1.28 to be fruitful and fill the earth. Hence, it is a good thing and part of God's economy that we have lots of different races and cultures. Genesis 11 dwells on the down-side of diversity, emphasizing how difference is not part of God's plan. It is, in effect, a punishment, and is responsible for misunderstanding and conflict. Genesis 10 is written by the group that thinks the problems of the world result from disharmony – of ignoring the big picture and neglecting the boundaries and interrelationships that God has put in place. The creation account in Genesis chapter 1 sets out the ideal for this group. Genesis 11, on the other hand, is written by a group that sees disobedience as the heart of the problem. The very different creation account in Genesis chapters 2 and 3 demonstrates their approach.*

The **second** thing to remember is that these are *stories* and not newspaper reports. They were not written to tell people what happened. They were written to persuade people of a truth that the authors wanted to have accepted. That sometimes means we have a bit of an obstacle to overcome, because in the western world generally we are not used to thinking about truth being conveyed through stories. We talk about facts, about what really happened and about evidence, and we can start to think that only that kind of truth matters. There is plenty of evidence of a different cultural approach. Aesop's fables are stories meant to convey moral truths. Jesus' parables challenge people to see the truth in a new way. Many cultures in different parts of the world tell stories about creation and about the origins of the nation to convey the truth about national identity and values. Modern novels, soap operas, and even reality TV shows can artificially produce situations in which truth is conveyed. Story is not a second best way of conveying truth. For some of the most profound truths it is better than evidence-based description. When talking about the things in which religion is interested, often we do not want to know what happened so much as whether and why it matters. We need to recognize and value the story-tellers' art.

And following from that, the **third** thing is that scholars are pretty sceptical about whether what we see in these books is a description of what really happened. It is difficult to either confirm or deny from the archaeological evidence, but the texts themselves are very confused, particularly as they describe the journeyings through the wilderness for 40 years. In Hebrew thought, the number 40 has a special significance. It is used in biblical writings wherever questions of vocation arise – that is when individuals or even nations are considering what they are called to be and do within God's purpose. In the Old Testament a number of people wander around for 40 days. In the New Testament Jesus himself spends 40 days in the wilderness. Here the people of Israel spend 40 years in the desert. The key question to ask is not: which years exactly were they? The key question is: what did they learn about their vocation? Again, the description of life set out in the Covenant agreement in Exodus

20—24, would have been unintelligible to fleeing slaves and desert nomads. Those chapters describe settled civic life in situations where law courts have been established, and where people have property and slaves of their own. The question to ask is not: Did it happen? The question is: Why did the authors choose to describe their origins in this way?

How can we use this material?

Here are some suggestions, based on specific Bible passages.

Read 📖 *Genesis 4.1–16. This is one of the stories describing 'the dilemma' about human experience from the section chapters 1—11 of Genesis. If we have heard this story at all, the likelihood is that we have accepted that Cain is 'the baddy' and that his crime involves not owning up to his guilt in killing his brother. In fact this is not the point of the story. The names of the brothers are interesting. In Hebrew, Cain means 'go-getter' and Abel means 'nothingness'. Cain seems to be doing everything right and he is the first to be mentioned as bringing a sacrifice to God. God inexplicably chooses Abel's sacrifice, and here is the heart of the problem – trying to understand God. If God had been even-handed there would have been no problem. He is the source of the problem. Also Cain's punishment is a strange one. He is banished from the idyllic setting in which he was prospering (just like his parents Adam and Eve) on account of his sin, but remains protected, and in a special category. This story introduces us to a theme and to questions we shall see later in the book of Job, and which belongs in any sophisticated description of creation. Why is life unfair, why is God not more transparent, where do humans stand with God? You might like to think about times when these have been questions for you. You might like to put God in the dock in the case of Cain and look at how the writer conducts his defence. Are you satisfied?*

Read 📖 *Genesis 17.1–22 and Genesis 35.9–15. These are all passages about name changes. Names are very important in Hebrew culture. To know someone's name is to know everything there is to know about them and to have power over them. That is why God never discloses his name fully. (He does tell Moses at Exodus 3.14 that he is called YHWH. In Hebrew that is a bit of a joke. It means 'I am what I am and I will be what I will be'.) These name changes mark promises. Abram (father of Ram, or High Father) becomes Abraham (father of a people or father of many). Sarai (laughing-stock) becomes Sarah (princess). Jacob (usurper, supplanted) becomes Israel (he who prevails with God). You might like to think of situations now where name changes or name giving are associated with promises (as for example at a wedding or a baptism). These names were charged with meaning. Is that how names are used today? What does your name mean? Does that have any bearing on the important things that mark you out as an individual? How do we deal with the information today, which was once contained in names?*

Read 📖 *Exodus 3.1–12. This describes the call of Moses. We have already read something of the call of Abram and of Jacob. Do you see any common themes here? Thinking of Jacob and Moses in particular, are they obvious choices for the job? Thinking of Moses especially, is his response enthusiastic? What does this tell you about the kind of people God calls to specific functions? Jacob was a twister and a cheat, and Moses was a murderer. Does this tell you anything new about God? Think of people that you have considered to be called by God. Do these stories help give your experience a different perspective?*

If you read the book of **Exodus** *through to* **chapter 15**, *you will see described a story about freeing slaves from a brutal oppressor. As we have seen, this experience was the first truly 'religious' experience for the whole people of Israel. It was the subject of the first 'creeds' or statements of belief. What do you consider to be an authentic religious experience? Would a liber-*

ation of this kind be high on the list? In the twentieth century especially, many Christians in places like South America were inspired by this story to 'rediscover' Christianity as a religion dedicated to freeing the poor and oppressed. Is this how you would describe the main aim of religion? How much sympathy do you have with those who describe liberation efforts in religious terms? Reflecting on this whole episode, what is the place of liberation thinking in your understanding of religion where you are? What do you think this account has to say to those who want to keep religion and politics separate?

Finally, it would be good to look at some laws. Read 📖 *Exodus chapters 21–23 (part of the so-called Book of the Covenant), and Leviticus 18 (part of the so-called Holiness Code). If we think of our two different approaches to 'the dilemma', the first passage is closer to the views of those who champion obedience as the answer. This Covenant sets out obligations of justice. The second passage is from those who think that keeping the correct boundaries and so maintaining holiness and purity as a means of maintaining harmony is the answer. Hence the long list of people with whom you shouldn't have sex. Does either of these ring a louder bell with you? Do you think it is legitimate to impose ethical rules on people who don't subscribe to the views that prompted them?*

Apart from giving us material for reflection, these passages do give us a flavour of the first few books of the Bible, and introduce us to some of their key themes. Accessible they may be. Simple, naïve, or irrelevant, they are not.

5

Getting Started on the
Old Testament History Books

What's included?

The Old Testament does not recognize the category 'history'. Its stories about the past are told for a purpose: to demonstrate the way in which God has related with his people in the past, so as to give guidance on how the relationship might work best in the present and future. That being said, one of the important and interesting things about the Old Testament is that it tells its stories about God against a background of people and events from the political and social life of the nation of Israel. This material is to be found in all three sections of the Hebrew Bible (Law, Prophets and Writings), but in Christian Bibles much of it has been grouped together.

The story that begins in Exodus is continued in the book of **Deuteronomy.** Most of that book is taken up with speeches or sermons of Moses, supposedly delivered to the people in the desert. At the very end of the book we have a report of Moses' death. He is to be succeeded as leader by Joshua.

The book of **Joshua** describes the conquest of the land of Canaan, the promised land, by the people of Israel. One famous passage in chapter 6 describes how Jericho was conquered, as the people marched round the city blowing trumpets. Much of the book describes how land was distributed amongst the 12 tribes. There is also some description of the uneasy relations with their neighbours. There is a sense of resolution and relief at the end of the book. The land is at peace, it has been distributed and organized, and once again the people have agreed to the terms of the covenant with God in a public declaration. The final chapter, 24, which contains details of that event, is the one you are most likely to hear read in churches.

Judges describes the uneasy move from taking over the land to establishing something that deserved the name civilization. At this time the guarantors of order were called Judges, hence the name of the book. They include relatively well-known figures like Samson and Gideon, and some of the most entertaining parts of the book include the folklore that had sprung up around them. Not all is plain sailing for this new nation however. They seem constantly to be involved in minor territorial wars in which they are not always successful. The authors offer their own commentary on this period. When the people do what is right and keep to the demands of the covenant, things go well for them. When they do evil, things go badly. The book pulls no punches in its descriptions of some of the debauched behaviour. There are passages in the book that you will never hear read publicly. A second piece of agenda concerns whether these judges are going to have sufficient authority and mandate to keep order and offer the right kind of strategic planning for the future. The authors plant in the readers' minds the idea that a king would be a better guarantee of morality and stability.

The *two books of* **Samuel** introduce us to a new class of religious functionary in Israel – the prophet. We see in these books the development of this role, or office, in its earliest stages. We see also the move towards establishing a monarchy and read about the reigns of two famous kings, Saul and David. There is more in the Bible about David than there is about Jesus. David is a very important figure still within Jewish culture. 2 Samuel describes the transition from David's rule to that of his successor Solomon. This section is one of the best reads in the Old Testament, recounted in the style and perhaps it could be said, with the same kind of agenda as a modern tabloid newspaper or celebrity magazine. David's personal life and that of his dysfunctional family come under the spotlight with no holds barred.

The books of **Kings** take the story on to the time of the Exile. It's a downhill slide, interesting politically, with lots of insights into the difficulties of making right choices when you're powerful. All the books mentioned so far are thought to come from the same party – a school of thought that you could call political or religious or both – with a view of the past that blames poor leadership for not controlling the people more effectively to maintain the demands of the covenant.

In Christian Bibles, these books are followed directly with *two books of* **Chronicles**. These are writings published at a later period, which tell essentially the same story as that we have just outlined. The first 9 chapters of 1 Chronicles is a way of telling history by listing the family trees of the people of Israel, with some additional comment in places. That's slightly less interesting than reading the phone book. After this, the narrative begins with the story of King Saul, though hardly any space is given to his exploits as described in the books of Samuel. We just hear about his death. This is clearly going to be a history that concentrates on David. In fact David's and Solomon's reigns are outlined in a much more serious tone, but using 2 Samuel and Kings as a source. 2 Chronicles ends with the conquest of Jerusalem and the beginning of the Exile.

The book of **Ezra** picks up the story from the end of the Exile and describes the return to Jerusalem, a story continued in **Nehemiah**. In these books, the building of a new temple is seen as a high priority and much of the narrative is given over to debate about that. The story ends on a high note with Nehemiah describing his achievements in a very positive way, as leaders often do.

For the first group of books especially, and to a lesser extent, the second, the theme of covenant is still very important. Land, as a religious theme is another important subject, and one that has resonance with modern world history. God is here portrayed at his most warlike and aggressive, though as we shall see, this picture cannot just be taken at face value and needs some unpacking.

What do we need to know to make sense of this?

One thing that the discipline of sociology has taught us is that history writing is never neutral. It is always from a point of view and always carries an agenda. Usually history is written from the point of view of the winners, and sociologists have lots of fun trying to work out what the losers might have said. In relation to Old Testament history there are no winners, though there may be voices that we're not hearing and it's always as well to bear that in mind – the voice of women is pretty muted for example. For the most part, this history has no corroborative evidence from sources outside the Old Testament itself, so we must be aware that we are only hearing the story as the teller wishes us to hear it, and as the teller understands the situation. Other explanations (as they say in TV listings magazine adverts) are possible. David, the great hero of the piece is mentioned nowhere outside the Bible. Mentions of the nation of Israel are limited to one or two disputed inscriptions.

What these books do present us with, however, are two different perspectives on events. Both perspectives are related to the questions raised by the trauma of the Exile, because, as we have seen, both histories reached their final form around the time of, and in response to, those times. The books from Deuteronomy to 2 Kings represent one perspective. The books from 1 Chronicles to Nehemiah represent the other. Each perspective results from asking slightly different questions. The question that prompted the first set of history books was: How could

God let this happen? The answer, alluded to above, is that the whole thing was the result of human disobedience and sin, compounded by weak leadership. The first group of books sets out to demonstrate that. That is one of the reasons why evil behaviour is described in such detail in Judges, for example; or why the lewd activities of David are dwelt upon. The additional agenda for this group is: 'Lessons must be learned. We must never allow this to happen again.'

The second set of books is also concerned with the future. Their authors want to build on lessons learned during exile. Their concern is that Israel needs to have an identity as a religious entity whether people live in the land of Israel or not. During the Exile they saw the things that strengthened that identity: the keeping of the Sabbath, male circumcision and the institutions and order of what you might call the civil/religious establishment. Their history gives much more respect to David's kingship, and describes Israel's rebuilding in very institutional terms. It is this same group that we came across in the last chapter that believed that disharmony, rather than disobedience was the problem. Their story of Israel emphasizes that view too, and loses no opportunity to promote circumcision and the Sabbath. When they look to the future, they speak of a newly purified land.

In order to follow the story, and especially to place individual snippets, it is helpful to have in mind the whole story of the history of Israel as it is told in these books. Once this would have been accepted as historical fact. Recently there has been quite a reaction against that, with some scholars claiming that the whole story is a fictional account. The majority view would probably be that historically reliable material is mixed in a creative way with material that is less reliable, to form an account that suits the aims of the writers. (It might be useful to reflect on how the stories of Robin Hood are used in contemporary culture, and how they contain a mixture of fact and legend.)

So what does this account tell us?

- Reading back from reliable dates, the date of the Exodus from Egypt would have been around the thirteenth or fourteenth century BCE.
- The date of 1000 BCE is usually given for the establishment of the kingdom of the whole of Israel under David.
- This kingdom continued under his and Solomon's rule until Solomon's death in 933 BCE.
- In the political chaos and power vacuum which accompanied the period after the death of Solomon, Israel effectively split into two different nations: one in the north called Israel with its capital Samaria, and one in the south called Judah with a capital in Jerusalem.
- In 721 BCE, the northern kingdom, Israel, was captured by one of the great regional powers, Assyria. We hear little about the history of the north thereafter. Most of our writings come from or describe the situation in Judah.
- Judah totters on as a tiny state in between much more powerful states for another hundred years or so, coming close to capture on occasion. But in 597 and 587 BCE in two waves of attacks Jerusalem falls to Babylonian forces and the people of Judah are taken into exile.
- In 538 BCE the Babylonian empire was conquered by the Persians, and the new king Cyrus decreed that the Judeans could return to Judah if they wished. Some did. Those who did not became the first members of the Jewish dispersion or Diaspora, living all over the Mediterranean world.

The stories about the conquest of the land, and its settlement have received lots of attention from scholars. Some believe that the account as we have it in Joshua and Judges is a credible account of what happened. An increasing number of scholars doubt that. The various accounts of the trek through the wilderness are difficult to reconcile with each other, and they include elements that are evidently literary devices. The references in the Covenant sections of Exodus clearly refer to a time and situation much later than that in the desert, and so must be regarded as something other than a record of fact. Archeological evidence does not support the account of the conquest in Judges. Perhaps most telling, there is increasing disquiet about the picture all this paints of God as some kind of bloodthirsty tyrant, quite prepared to sanction ethnic cleansing on a whim. This does not accord with anything we learn about God elsewhere in the Bible. In fact, what seems at present to be the most likely theory about what really happened is something like this: The people who came to be described as 'Israelites', were actually people who lived in the more oppressed classes of Canaanite society. They were joined by escaped slaves from Egypt who brought with them stories of a liberator God and between them they engineered a kind of Peasants' Revolt to overthrow unjust and oppressive Canaanite rulers.

What this points to is this: Asking the question, 'What happened?' is probably misguided and unhelpful. More helpful is the question, 'Why did they decide to describe it like this?' That takes us back to the questions about agenda, and reminds us what the authors of Deuteronomy, Joshua and Judges want us to conclude. That is:

• God's gift is wonderful.
• God's people effectively threw it back in God's face by neglecting the entirely justified demands that went with it.
• God had every right to be angry and to exercise his considerable power to teach Israel a lesson.

Also, in the wider question about how optimistic a view of humankind we can have, they want us to conclude that:

• Humankind's fatal flaws need strong control if they are not to overwhelm God's goodness.
• Good kings can provide that.
• Bad kings are the worst of all worlds.

And that lessons need to be learned if the tragedy of the Exile is to be avoided in the future.

What we are presented with, then, is a cautionary tale, exaggerated for the sake of effect, directed towards teaching people after the Exile that they must restore justice and obedience, as the Covenant demands, if there is to be peace.

It may be more helpful to approach the accounts as if we were approaching pieces of creative literature, rather than historical documents of record.

How can we use this material?

Read 📖 *2 Samuel chapter 11. This is one of those bits of tabloid journalism noted above. Read this as a piece of story-telling and consider this story-tellers' art. The style is almost jaunty, in a way that highlights the scandal. See where the details occur that give the story its interest. Note how closely human nature has been observed here. For instance, look at how David's anger subsides between verse 22 and verse 25, as soon as he realizes how the campaign has been organized so as to get rid of poor old loyal Uriah. If you want to see how the authors of the other history deal with this period in their story, read* 📖 *1 Chronicles 20.1.*

Here, biography is being used as a means of religious teaching and learning. How effective do you think that is? Why do you read the life stories of other people? Is it just because they are interesting, or is it because they are in some way, inspiring? Think of any biography that has had an effect on you. Now think about how we might best teach people about religion today. Should we tell inspiring stories of Jesus, or stories about people who have been inspired by him, or is it better to abandon biography and present people with doctrines and arguments in a different or more theoretical way? What is the most effective thing about this passage – what does it teach? Can you think of a better way of making the same point?

Read 📖 Joshua chapter 7. This chapter describes an incident during the conquest of the land, in which Israel is unsuccessful in capturing the town of Ai. The reason is God's justified anger against someone called Achan who has been disobedient. On the face of it, there is little forgiveness, grace or gentleness evident in this passage, which paints an unattractive picture of a vengeful and easily offended God. But is that fair? Bearing in mind the agendas of the writers, what do you think is the point of this story? Can you imagine a different way of describing these events, which simply dealt with 'the facts'? What would be the difference between them? Does looking at the passage in this way help you to form a strategy for reading accounts like this?

This overall story is of a people whose identity is bound up with the belief that they have been given a land by God. What are the plusses and minuses of believing that, for the people concerned?

On the plus side *you might think of the possibilities that belief offers in terms of humility. If the land was a gift rather than something they won or had an indigenous right to, then that might promote attitudes of gratefulness and offer a model of gifting which could influence all parts of society. That is certainly the vision of Deuteronomy and the history stories, which come from that school, including Joshua through to 2 Kings.*

On the other hand, *such a belief could lead to arrogant disdain of normal political life and a siege mentality, which seems to have happened at various times in the history of this nation. You might think of:*

- *situations in the world today in which a particular people believes it has a land by divine right;*
- *whether such beliefs, in practice, have been helpful to world peace and stability or not;*
- *how countries that hold such beliefs are viewed by other countries;*
- *whether these accounts are capable of being used to interpret that belief in a useful way today.*

Read 📖 *1 Samuel 9.1—10.1. This is an account of how Saul became Israel's first king. It's a very positive account and you will be left thinking that it is certainly part of God's design that Israel should have a king. Now* **read** 📖 **the preceding chapter 8.** *Confused? This chapter sets out all the objections to having a king. God is enough of a leader. Any human leader will be flawed. What do you make of these two accounts being next to each other? It's worth recalling that the Bible often presents us with alternative views and invites us to make up our own minds. Now* **read** 📖 *1 Kings 4.20–34. At first sight this looks like a piece of writing to praise king Solomon. But what if it were written with a degree of irony? Could it be said that the predictions of 1 Samuel 8 were being fulfilled here – and remember what comes next: the breakup of the kingdom and its decline? What do you think we are being asked to believe about kingship? Does this have anything to say about modern politics?*

Read 📖 *2 Kings 22.1–13. Here, for a change, is a king about whom the authors have nothing bad to say. Perhaps the reason is that this king, Josiah, is closely associated with the party that is writing the story! He was a reformer, and the account in this passage tries to build a story around his reforms. A scroll was discovered in the temple and suddenly everything must be reassessed. (That sounds like something out of a Dan Brown novel.) What happened was that a group of religious radicals, whom we assume are responsible for the book of Deuteronomy and the history books which immediately follow it, set about redefining and reordering religion, in order to rescue it from obscurity and decline. Lots of outlying shrines were closed down. There was (probably) one centre of excellence at Jerusalem. A new responsibility was placed on parents to educate their children in religion, with a new emphasis on the home as the place where religion is to be honoured and practised. Are there any parallels in today's world? What is the place of religious radicalism? Should societies that have all but abandoned religion by denying it anything other than lip service have religion re-introduced? What does it bring to a society that has rejected it? All these books, and the ones we shall look at next, attempt to grapple with those questions.*

Read 📖 Judges 19.16–26. This is one of the passages you will not hear read publicly. It's a terrible tale of depravity. There are possible reasons for including it here that are to do with later attitudes towards Gibeah. For our purposes, and partly as an introduction to the next section, reflect on what, if anything, moral attitudes and behaviour tell us about a society's health and wholeness. Are the writers correct to provide this sort of thing as evidence that 'something must be done'?

The history books tell us about a God who is known within the social and political life of a nation, and who is at least partly defined by the Covenant agreement – this is the kind of God he is. Beyond that, these stories serve the different agendas of those who are trying to discover what it might mean to be truly religious in their own times.

6

Getting Started on the Prophets

There is a section of the Hebrew Bible called 'Prophets'. It is divided into two sub-sections: the Former Prophets, and (as you might expect) the Latter Prophets. Rather confusingly, the books that are described in the first sub-section, we have already dealt with as 'history books'. They are the books from Joshua through to 2 Kings. In Christian Bibles the prophets section comes right at the end of the Old Testament, and mostly contains books from the Latter Prophets section of the Hebrew Bible.

What's included?

By far the longest books in this section are the first three: **Isaiah, Jeremiah** and **Ezekiel**. Each of these books is a mixture, on the one hand, of narrative story-telling, usually about the exploits of the prophet in question, though often with a political or social context, and on the other, series of prophetic sayings. These sayings are usually known by the more formal name, oracles. They purport to be the direct word of God delivered by the prophet in specific situations, delivered sometimes to individuals and sometimes to specific groups or even, more rhetorically, to nations. They often begin with the words, 'thus says Yahweh' (or 'thus says the Lord', depending on your translation).

Some of the best-known passages in the Old Testament come from the book of **Isaiah**. Those familiar with Handel's *Messiah* will recognize the opening paragraphs of chapter 40. Those familiar with services of Nine Lessons and Carols will be familiar with parts of chapters 7, 9 and 11. Chapter 53 is one of the most popular readings for Good Friday. This book is often quoted in the New Testament. Jesus' first recorded 'sermon' in Luke 4.18 and 19, for example, takes a text from Isaiah chapter 61. The book of Isaiah as it appears in our Bibles is normally considered to be a kind of third edition. The first edition is roughly chapters 1—39. The second edition extends that with new chapters 40—55, and the final edition extends it even further from 56 to 66. Each of these editions and additions is associated with a different period in Israel's history.

We have a few clues about the original prophet Isaiah from the book, but we find the book of **Jeremiah** far more revealing about its author. The book contains a number of what we would now call 'video diary' pieces, which give us an insight into the prophet's private thoughts. He was working at a time when things were going very badly. He was speaking, by and large, to people who were in denial about the seriousness of the situation, and for whom the easiest thing was to turn their anger on the messenger. Indeed, he was personally attacked and abused, as well as being ignored, so it's not surprising that his book is pretty dark and woeful. It does contain one section of more hopeful or positive material (chapters 29—33). **Ezekiel** has been the subject of much study and speculation on account of the bizarre nature of some of his visions, which are said to border on the obscene. (Do not read chapters 16 or 23 if you are of a nervous disposition or easily offended.) One scholar thinks he is suffering from post-traumatic stress disorder! His book, too, contains an account of his call as a prophet and deals with reconstruction of the nation after the Exile. In particular, he is keen to stress personal moral responsibility. He does not agree with the popular motto of the time: 'The fathers have eaten sour grapes and the children's teeth are set on edge.'

The remaining books are usually quite short, and consist mostly of oracles, though sometimes with a little biographical material, usually related to the call of the prophet named, or the context of their utterance. The ones you are most likely to encounter from readings in church are:

- **Amos and Micah,** who have memorable things to say about justice;
- **Hosea,** whose prophecy is closely associated with his own life story in which he marries someone who is consistently unfaithful to him;
- **Haggai,** whose prophecies are about the building of the temple after the Exile, and so find resonance with those celebrating new building projects or anniversaries of old ones;
- **Malachi,** a series of oracles that seem naturally to lead to the New Testament and arrival of Jesus, and so are read around Christmas. Some phrases from his speeches feature in Christmas carols (e.g. 'Risen with healing in his wings');
- **Jonah,** whose acquaintance with a whale is one of the best-known of all Bible stories.

In Christian Bibles, **Daniel** is included in this section. Strictly speaking this is not a prophetic book. It is part of the 'Writings' section of the Hebrew Bible. It does contain some similarities with prophetic works but actually it is an example of a specific kind of literature called apocalyptic, which is designed to be *read*, as opposed to prophetic works that are reports of oracles meant to be spoken and heard. The rest of these short books are rarely read and some are barely intelligible without much more background material.

What do we need to know to make sense of this material?

The first thing we need to sort out is: What is a prophet? Perhaps even more importantly, we need to know what a prophet is not. The former prophet books tell us something about the development and growth of the role of prophet, through telling us about unnamed prophets, and prophet-like figures that have a walk-on part in stories of more important people, like Saul. Samuel, Elijah and Elisha all display prophet characteristics, and through their stories we see how 'true' prophets are distinguished from 'false' ones, so defining this class of people better.

In the early days, prophets were basically consultants. If you wanted to know the answer to some conundrum, you visited them and possibly, paid them. They might then go into some kind of trance helped by music or drugs before giving you an answer.

Groups of these people apparently gathered around kings, as policy consultants. From the accounts we read it seems that they were very aware of who employed them, and they were very wary of giving bad news or critical judgement. The source of their inspiration is usually portrayed in the Old Testament as untrustworthy and spurious.

Of course, the authors who wanted to blame kings for bad leadership thought of these court prophets as equally to blame and they are contrasted very unfavourably with true prophets of Yahweh (or the Lord) who are not afraid to give bad news, do it for free, and often do it quite reluctantly. Being a true Yahweh prophet is not something you choose as a career option. God chooses you, and this is often very inconvenient for the people concerned. In the same way you do not choose to be the recipient of an oracle, on some sort of consultancy basis. If God has something to say to you, he tells you, whether you're ready to hear it or not.

In the early days, prophets are consulted to see what will happen in the future. As the role matures, oracles are more concerned with offering commentary on the present. Of course, the difference can be quite subtle. 'If (or perhaps, because) you continue with this policy, disaster will follow', is both commentary on the present and a foretelling of the future.

The great prophets who have books named after them are counter-cultural and answerable only to God. They are party to what might be called the heavenly councils. As one modern writer puts it, they share God's dreams and his nightmares.

Since the prophetic books are contextual – that is they record oracles that were delivered to specific situations – if we are to make sense of them we need to know something about the situations that are addressed. There are limits to what we can know, since some of the detail is only available from a between the lines reading of the prophets' own work, and we can't be sure that we are getting a balanced view. But we are able to relate the books to backgrounds to a degree, and this is generally thought to be an essential piece of background for full understanding.

Prophets of the eighth century BCE are speaking to a relatively settled and comfortable society that has difficulty recognizing that, either, it has need for religious appraisal, or, there is anything seriously wrong. **Amos, Micah, Hosea** and **Isaiah 1—39** belong to this period. They have varying emphases but, overall, their message is that the covenant demands of justice and righteousness are being neglected, and that the lack of religious and moral values at the heart of society will prove to be its downfall.

Prophets of the seventh century BCE include **Nahum, Zephaniah, Habakkuk** and, most importantly, **Jeremiah**. They are prophesying at a time of impending doom, just before the Exile, at a time of great anxiety, when the nation really doesn't know its house of prayer from its elbow. Their role is to get people to accept reality, and to begin the process of reflection about how this has all come about.

Ezekiel and **Isaiah 40—55** are the main sixth-century prophets – voices from within the exiled community. They stand on the cusp between explanations of disaster and assurances for the future. The people will return. God will forgive. There is a future and a new way to be a religious person based on the new things people believe they have learned about God in the Exile experience. Most notably this has suggested to them, that there is only one God, creator and designer of the world, its history and all its peoples.

The main post-Exile prophets are **Haggai, Zechariah** and **Isaiah 56—66**. Their prophecies are about the restored nation back in their own land.

It's important to remember that there was a close connection between some of the history story writers and some of the prophets. For some of the time, some of them were, in effect, working together. There are very strong idealistic links, for example, between Jeremiah and Deuteronomy, or between the Chronicler's history story and the prophecies of Ezekiel. There are links between the thinking of Isaiah 40—55 and Leviticus, and between the eighth-century prophets and the books of Samuel and Kings. Because these books are arranged in the way they are in our Bibles, we can miss these connections. It is in the words of the prophets that we can sometimes discern the agendas of the story writers.

One thing not to forget is that prophets could be seen as a threat by those who regarded themselves as the guardians of the tradition. If we want to know what God says now, who holds the authority, and therefore the power, to speak for him? Is it those who have treasured the stories and traditions of the faith and nurtured its institutions, or is it those who claim to speak for God directly in the present and who bypass all that? This question represents a real tension between prophets and priests, which is not even resolved at the time of the New Testament, or perhaps even today.

A final thing to bear in mind, related to that is this. In the Old Testament we have already seen a number of tensions between opposing views about religion, society and life. The prophets sharpen one of those tensions. An important strand of Old Testament thinking values order, and the institutions that guarantee that. At times (for example, in 2 Samuel 7) we can see how God is linked with the 'establishment' made up of kings and priests, and especially with 'the house of David'. Prophets represent an alternative strand, which is quite subversive in that it gives a voice to the poor, the powerless, the pained, the outsider, widow, orphan, and the dispossessed. The Covenant in Exodus 20 is with all the people. It is 'a people's covenant' and has a bottom-up emphasis that gives attention to those whom the establishment can disregard or who can be its victims. The prophets stand with this subversive strand. They remind the powerful of their responsibilities and call them to judgement. This comparison is sometimes used as a way of understanding the tradition in which Jesus stands, seeing Jesus and John the Baptist as following the prophetic tradition, and the religious Jewish establishment of Sadducees following the priestly tradition of privilege.

How can we use this material?

The most popular use of prophetic material in reflection, is as a tool with which to critique society today.

*To get the feel of the work of eighth century prophets **read** 📖 Amos 6.1–7 together with 2.6–11. Do you get the picture? The question as to how accurate a picture this is of society then is really irrelevant, since most of us will be able to recognize it now. The picture is of a society that sees no need for religion. Festivals have lost their meaning and the observance of ancient religious customs just gets in the way of business (8.5–7). Religion and morality have become separated. Contemporaries like Isaiah believe society has lost a sense of God's holiness, and so lost something of the whole concept of sanctity. Hosea detects a society that does not have love and relationship at its heart. How important are these things? How do you judge them to be present and active? What would a society look like that honoured them? Does that present an attractive picture, and is it worth yearning, praying and working for? Many generations of Christians have been inspired by just this kind of reflection. Can you understand why this should be? If you get a chance, try and get hold of a copy of Martin Luther King's 'I have a dream' speech. Trace the similarities between the cadences of that, and these prophetic writings.*

Now read something from the seventh century. **Read** 📖 *Jeremiah 6.9–15*. This is a word of judgement against those who have not understood the root causes of their problems, and are in denial about their seriousness. Priests and (false) prophets are included in the indictment. Elsewhere (for example, 44.15–30) we see how a climate of anxiety allied with a superficial, almost superstitious view of religion leads people to strange securities, including pagan rites. Are there any parallels that you see in today's society? Is there any voice that you can discern like that of Jeremiah? Would it be appropriate for there to be one?

As a sixth-century piece, *read* 📖 *Isaiah 40.1–11*. There comes a time when the blaming has to stop and the looking forward has to begin. It's at that point that we can really begin to talk about a theology of failure. What has our tragedy taught us about God? There must be new things to learn, because what we thought we knew about God is inadequate to make sense of our situation now. Isaiah draws a big picture of God. No longer is the nation of Israel his only interest. Rather, he is interested in the whole of creation and in the peoples of the whole world and their destiny. This passage also introduces the relatively new concept of forgiveness, as a means of coping with the new situation and giving permission to be hopeful rather than blame obsessed. That gives us plenty to reflect on.

- Can you think of times when there has been a huge change in your understanding of the world? Was that connected with suffering or tragedy? What were the relative roles of pain and hope as you came to terms with that new understanding and is there anything in this passage that reminds you of that?
- What do you think is the most effective way to deal with the mistakes of the past: blame or forgiveness? What are the relative merits of each?
- How 'national' is your view of God, if you have one? How difficult is it to think of a God of the whole world? What are the advantages?

*An example of post-exilic prophecy would be 📖 **Haggai**
1.2–11. This prophet is closely associated with the priestly
approach that also lies behind books like Chronicles, Ezra and
Leviticus. These people believed that for religious and communal life to succeed in the future, and for the distinctive identity
of the people of Israel to be maintained, even in dispersion,
there needed to be an honouring of institutions like the Sabbath
and male circumcision, and a new emphasis on restoring purity
to the land, with a focus on holiness. In practical terms this
meant that rebuilding the temple was a priority for them.
Nothing else is going to work unless and until that happens.
This passage sets out that view clearly. The way of thinking that
lies behind the passage is less well understood than those that
call for a return to the covenant demands for justice and righteousness, though they are not necessarily mutually exclusive.
The approach is sometimes called 'sacramental', a term used
in churches today as a way of describing God's presence in
mundane things, and the importance of having ceremonies and
symbols which declare that. You might want to reflect:*

- *Do we need churches at all? Do all these ceremonies and rules
and regulations get in the way of the important things? Or is
it rather that they are an essential part of reminding us about
the important things, and most of all, of the presence of God
in our midst now?*
- *What do the terms 'holiness' and 'purity' mean to you? In
your experience do they point to positive or negative things?*
- *What are the things that give religion an identity? Is it the
ceremonies and customs or something else? In the New
Testament, customs and religious rules generally get a bad
press, as they are thought to have become empty of real
meaning. How can that be prevented and should we try?*

*According to the singer/song writer, Paul Simon, 'the words of
the prophets are written on the subway walls and tenement
halls'. Where, if anywhere do you think they can be found?
Having seen the role of prophets in Old Testament society, how
would you recognize prophets in your own? Would they be:*

- *People who stand out because their views are so 'off the wall' and at odds with what most people think, or*
- *People who attract a huge following and whose words are remembered, or*
- *People who speak from a religious perspective offering a moral and spiritual commentary on life, or*
- *Other kinds of secular commentator?*

Each of the following people has at some time been called a prophet. Is there anything in common between them and the prophets of the Bible?

- *Lord Longford*
- *Bishop Tutu*
- *E.F. Schumacher (author of a book about sustainable economic growth called* Small is Beautiful)
- *Andy Warhol*
- *John Lennon*

If none of these is satisfactory can you add your own?

The prophets have a very special role in Bible writing. They remind the religious community how the practice of religion in society should operate. They witness to a God who is still interested and involved in the world, and show, subversively, that God's will can be accessed outside the tradition holders, if they start to act as gatekeepers. Their message is one of both judgement and hope. It is delivered to 'church' and nation. It embraces the national and the international. Through reading the prophets we have an additional insight into what 'a man or woman of God' can look like, and what a religious life truly involves.

7

Getting Started on Psalms,
Proverbs and Job

Proverbs and Job belong to what in Christian Bibles is sometimes known as the 'Wisdom' section. There is no such section
in the Hebrew Bible where these two books are to be found in
the third and latest, 'Writings' section. The two books are quite
unlike each other at first sight, but on closer inspection they do
have enough in common to look at them together. Most fundamentally, they both deal with different aspects of what we are
going to call 'creation theology' (on which, more later). That is
their link with the book of Psalms, which is also among the
Writings, though we'd have to say it's a book unlike any other
in the Bible.

What's included?

The book of **Psalms** looks like a hymn-book without an index.
It contains materials for worship in various situations and for
different groups of people. Some of the main scholarly work on
this book has been to try and organize the various psalms under
sensible headings. Those who have done so have recognized
that some psalms appear to be for individual and some for communal use, though the prevailing wisdom is that all were actually used in communal worship. (Nowadays in some churches
where a corporate confession of faith is made, although everyone does it, it still begins 'I believe'.) The most common type of

psalm is the lament, a way of pouring out grief, describing pain, complaining about the injustice of life, and wondering where God is in all this. But there are also hymns of celebration, some of which are obviously linked to specific happy occasions, such as a wedding (Psalm 45), a pilgrimage to Jerusalem on a significant occasion (Psalm 122), or a coronation (Psalm 99).

The book of Psalms is actually divided into five, but there is no evidence that that division is significant for understanding the book and its contents. There are also groupings of Psalms with a common theme or common vocabulary (for example, Psalms 113—118 all include the word 'Hallelujah' – Let the Lord's Name be Praised – and the sentiments associated with that). Most readers, however, are content to dip into the book and read the psalms as unconnected pieces of poetry or devotion. That may be to underestimate them. If these are communal and public pieces of worship and liturgy, then they do represent an attempt to put into words what it meant to real people to believe in God or to have religious faith in situations that are still recognizable. In Christian churches today, worship at its best is not insignificant. It is constantly changing as new attempts are made to understand what God does in the world and in human life. It reflects a theological quest, and should be a way of accessing the self-understanding of the religious community.

Many people's contact with the Psalms is through those more modern Christian hymns that are a re-working of the ancient texts. Isaac Watts, sometimes called the father of modern hymnody, was responsible for re-writing many Psalms to make them suitable for metrical singing. Examples include: 'O God our Help in Ages Past' (Psalm 90) and 'Jesus Shall Reign Where'er the Sun' (Psalm 72), as well as lesser-known hymns based on Psalms 19, 84, 119 and 136. 'The Lord's my Shepherd, I'll not Want' is a well-known metrical version of Psalm 23, and 'All People that on Earth do Dwell' is similarly based on Psalm 100.

The book of **Proverbs** is a series of pithy observations about the human condition, and about human relations and behaviour. It is framed primarily as advice to young men about how to behave in order to belong properly to society, and in the process gives us many clues about how the writers perceived society, at its best, to operate. They set out a world view in which to be focused on self-improvement is not at odds with living a spiritual life, and in which living a healthy and successful life is seen as co-operating with God's creative will. Solomon is often taken as the epitome of wisdom, and his great wealth was but further evidence of that. This world view is constructed around the concept of wisdom – an idea that encompasses everything worthwhile, creative and to be strived for. Wisdom is evidence of God's current activity in the world and, as such, is to be embraced. There are eight different terms for 'fool' in this book and you wouldn't want any of them to be applied to you.

The most important institution of society is the family, and so sexual misbehaviour is especially condemned as it threatens this security. In rather bizarre fashion, young men are portrayed as being vulnerable to the wiles of scheming women who want to rob them of their virtue. Women are generally portrayed as (useful or even indispensable) adjuncts to men. The good wife is particularly to be sought. The nagging wife is particularly to be dreaded. A good woman enhances a man's reputation and standing in society. A poor wife makes a fool of her husband. Yet, ironically, in chapters 8 and 9, Wisdom is portrayed as female. The subordination of passion is a good thing, and self-control is a sign of maturity. When all else fails within the family, corporal punishment is encouraged in the task of education. The things to be avoided are adulterers and adultery, drunkenness (because of the lack of self-control involved), idleness, gossip and a nagging wife. Life itself is seen as good, and death is a taboo subject. You may wonder why such a mundane collection of sayings and observations can be included in the same book as the great poetic prophecies of Isaiah or the exciting and significant story of the Exodus. In fact, as we shall see, there is good and interesting theological reason.

No such question would be asked about the book of **Job** – for many people perhaps the most profound of all the books of the Old Testament. In a sense this is odd because, unlike so many other Old Testament books, it makes no pretence at being a piece of history. It presents itself as a piece of fiction. Indeed, the opening lines amount to 'Once upon a time in a land far away'. There is something quite modern about the way Job operates as a piece of communication. We might think of it as a rather formal play, rather like a mystery play or some other medieval play like *Everyman* in which characters represent points of view and the play functions as a means of giving them a hearing and consideration. It is possible even to compare it with modern soap opera or even reality TV. As a story, it depends upon the audience, the reader, knowing something that the cast do not know. From the beginning the reader is taken into the narrator's confidence as the story unfolds. The narrative, story-telling sections are very short as a proportion of the book overall. Most of the book is given over to the long and poetic speeches of the main characters.

The story, contained in the first two chapters, is about a wager in heaven. You have to imagine heaven as a remote place, organized on very formal lines, in which decisions are made that influence the world. These decisions are made by what we might now call cabinet ministers. The prime minister is God. There is one minister without portfolio whose name is (the) Satan. The wager is between God and Satan. God is very proud of an upright man called Job, who is the very model of a devout religious person. He does everything right according to the standards of the day as set out in the book of Proverbs or indeed in Job chapter 31. Satan tells God that Job is only good because of the advantages it has brought him. Indeed he has done well, but then that is surely (according to the inherited beliefs of the times) a sign of living a good life. God tells Satan that Job's goodness is less selfish than that. So he 'allows' Satan to strip Job of all his wealth and possessions and even of his family, in order to prove that Job will still remain faithful, even in adversity. Having done so, God is proved right, but Satan is not satisfied. In this first wager there was a condition. Job must not suffer personal injury. Were he to do so, argues Satan, then it would be a different story. So God 'allows' that too. Once again he is proved correct. Job will not curse God even though (in a great story-telling detail) he is urged to do so by his nagging wife, after finding himself covered in a mass of running sores.

Thereafter the main characters are introduced, and we hear no more about Satan or the wager. There are three main characters and most of the book is taken up with their speeches. Each represents a particular point of view. The issue with which they are dealing is a modern and pressing one. What sense can we make of religious faith when bad things happen to good people? Each of the three has in common a view that there is justice in the world, and that good fortune and ill fortune are somehow tied up with what people deserve. They want to hang on to the idea that good people inevitably prosper and bad people inevitably pay the price for that. Job's experience is the experience of many. Life appears to them to have come from the hand of a God who plays with them, and seems to have nothing at all to do with the kind of person one is, or the kind of life one leads. What's the point of religion then, and what on earth can faith mean? Holding the view of Job's colleagues means arguing that Job must deserve his fate (something the reader knows is rubbish). Each of the three puts a convincing case why Job must be wrong and they must be correct. The list includes: their own experience in the past, having a vision from God that tells them they're right, the tradition of the forefathers, and studying modern theology. All of these tell them that Job must have done something wrong. Over against this is Job's own experience. He knows (as does the reader) that he has done nothing wrong, and refuses to give his three friends satisfaction. In the end, God himself re-enters as a character and Job is vindicated. This leaves readers in the position of having to re-think their own position in relation to the issues addressed.

What do we need to know to make sense of this material?

In order to connect with the books of Proverbs and Job we have to put ourselves in the position of people whose world view has changed radically. On the negative side, the Exile had been experienced by Israel not just as a national disaster but also as a crisis for religious faith. Any understanding that God had a special relationship with this people, and that he had promised them a land and descendants for ever, was completely destroyed as Israel was overcome and its people taken captive in Babylon. The book of Job is not just asking the personal question, 'Why do bad things happen to good people?' It is asking the further question: 'If bad things consistently happen to good people, is there any sense at all in which religious faith is still valid?'

But there was also a positive side. As long as the people of Israel lived within their own borders they could consider their God YHWH to be one god among many. True, he might be the best and strongest god – and there are accounts of some trials of strength in some of the earlier books – but he is held within the limits of the boundaries of Israel and his interest only extends there. Once the Exile happened all that changed. According to the prophets, God was with his people in Babylon, as much as he had been in Israel. It was God who was organizing the political drama with an international cast that would lead to the end of the Exile and the return to their own land. Slowly, people began to think the hitherto unthinkable – that there was only one God and that that God was YHWH. But that too was an idea that had implications that needed to be thought through.

In particular, if God were the one God then he must have been the creator of the world, and if creator of the natural world, then he must have created the world of social relations, politics and history too. This was a huge thought with both a positive and a negative side. The positive side was that there now opened up a whole new way of knowing God. If God were the creator then it should be possible to know something of God from observing his creation. If everything worked well, then this must mean that humankind had correctly interpreted God's will and co-operated with it. This is the theological basis of the book of Proverbs. It could be subtitled: 'finding out about God by exploring what he's done'. It's one way in which you could say religion meets science.

On the other hand, if God were the creator of the world, why had he not made a better job of it? Why was the world such a hostile place for humankind? Why was there natural disaster? Why were there dangerous animals and hostile environments? Why was there war? Why did God allow injustice? Why did he allow any kind of suffering at all? Surely in an ideal creation these things would be done away with, or have no place. The book of Job begins to open the possibility of asking these questions. Presumably, they were asked by those whose faith had been destroyed, as well as by those who wanted to continue somehow to hold religious faith. And in other later books of the Old Testament we see how some writers developed and responded to these questions. Among the answers they came up with were these.

- God has designed history in a sequence of ages. Suffering by good people in this age will be rewarded in the next.
- Just as there was once a kingdom of Israel, so in another age there will be a new kingdom in which God's rule is complete. This will be like a whole new creation, heralded perhaps by a new anointed one (messiah) like David.
- Suffering can be used by God for a purpose. One person's suffering can actually achieve something worthwhile. It can be redemptive.
- Suffering is somehow still to do with sin and disharmony. The way to cope with suffering is to cope with sin.

Some of these ideas were further developed and re-thought in the New Testament and particularly as a way to describe theologically and make sense of, the death of Jesus.

The conclusion of Job is that God is somehow to be found in the midst of suffering. To come close to God is somehow to come close to grief. This too is a discernible strand in New Testament thinking.

So how do the Psalms fit into this picture? Some scholars think that in the Psalms we can see the movement in people's thinking from a simple creation theology that says: God is good, life is wonderful, and the reason that I'm so successful is that I'm so religious; to something more profound and realistic. On the one hand, the largest category of Psalms is that of laments. There is a whole huge section of Psalms that express just the sort of grief we've been describing – the awfulness of coming to terms with a world in which suffering seems to have no reason or purpose, and in which the God in whom you trusted seems impotent. Beyond that, it is claimed that there are Psalms which move beyond that, to a new mature faith in which life is once more worthwhile and good.

How can we use this material?

Perhaps the most useful way of reflecting on this material altogether is to try to picture the kinds of people responsible for the writings and to see if we can see their equivalents in our own society – even perhaps if we can identify with them, or react against them.

It is interesting, for example, to try to trace that movement from happy optimism, through disillusion to a new realization of faith and hope, in the Psalms. If you want to try that, start with reading 📖 Psalm 33. Imagine the kind of person nowadays for whom this might strike a chord. What kind of income might they have? Where would they live? What newspaper would they read? Note how creation theology has its downside. It always favours the status quo. 'God created it like this. It works for me, so it should stay like this.' The apartheid regime in South Africa was justified using creation theology. Next, you might look at Psalm 74. What is the author angry about? Can you identify with him at all? Do you think he wants to have faith? An example of what you might call reconstituted faith could be Psalm 30 or 32. These Psalms tell the story of the movement from naïve faith, through disaster and despair to a new kind of faith. Does this movement speak to you at all. Do you recognize your own place in this scheme?

You might reflect on the place of public worship in Christianity. How important is it to publicly declare what we believe, or to publicly question God in a subversive way, or to share our hopes and fears in a way that some might even find embarrassing? What kind of things should hymns be about, and how much impression do words make? If you sing hymns, do you remember the words or the tune?

It's been suggested that the book of Psalms is like a score for 'Israel – the Musical' bringing together in a popular way and in a particular idiom, some of the key experiences which went to make up the identity of this people. If you had to write a show entitled 'God – the Musical' what would it be about?

Continuing the task of trying to imagine what an author is like, look at 📖 Proverbs 23.22 and read through to 24.34. Can you identify the characteristics noted above? What kind of person would have written this? Think about the gender, family circumstances, age and social standing of the author. What is at stake for them here? How central is this kind of thing to religious profession do you think?

The easiest parts of the book of Job to access are the story introduction in chapters 1 and 2, and then the initial speeches from the friends in chapters 4, 8 and 11. Imagine yourself in Job's position. Would you have been any more convinced than him? Is this a good way of setting the questions about suffering, justice and faith, do you think? If there were one problem you might like to explore with this structure how would you write a story or devise a TV programme with the title 'Playing God'?

The Wisdom writers grapple with modern questions about human existence and the place of faith. They connect with modern experience at a point where old certainties are being tested against experience, and where life has reached a stage where permission is being sought to think in new and hitherto unimaginable ways.

8

Getting Started on the Lesser Known Books of the Old Testament

Lesser known does not necessarily mean less important, and the books we shall consider here are those, which, although less often read in services or quoted in sermons are nevertheless interesting and important. Being lesser known is mostly what they have in common, though they do include a collection of five short works which are each designed to be read at particular Jewish festivals – a custom that survives to this day.

What's included?

The book of **Ruth** is a drama in six scenes that explores a series of close relationships, and in the process examines something of the link between power and weakness in those relationships. Part of the action is set at harvest time and this scroll is read at a Jewish harvest festival. It is a controversial work because of the implied comments and statements it makes about the relationship between Israelites and foreigners. This culminates in the claim that even the iconic Hebrew figure, David, had foreign blood in his veins. The story that this book tells is of a woman named Ruth, from the foreign and unpopular nation of Moab, who marries an Israelite, and becomes in all respects a much-loved member of his family. However, her husband dies, and the bereaved family set off from Moab back to their ancestral home of Bethlehem. Her mother-in-law, foreseeing the problems she might have, urges Ruth to return to her own country and her own people, but she refuses, insisting on remaining to support her mother-in-law. In Bethlehem it is harvest time and we have a brief account of how Ruth meets a suitor while working as a harvester in the fields. This man, Boaz, regularizes his relationship with her, marries her and she bears a son to whom Naomi the mother-in-law becomes foster mother. So, in a Mills and Boon kind of way, all ends very happily. The further significance is in the final verses of this short book. Ruth's half-caste son is called Obed. He becomes the father of Jesse who in turn becomes the father of David.

The book of **Esther** also reads like a novel but it has a different setting. It's more *Sex and the City* than Mills and Boon. This novel is about the plight of Jews after the Exile and dispersion, living in the Persian Empire. As has been the experience of Jews in many such situations throughout history, they were vulnerable, sometimes persecuted, and their situation was precarious. The story concerns a plot against the Jews, which is not only foiled, but which sees the chief plotter hoist by his own petard. The style of the book is lively and darkly comic, at times descending into farce. Like Ruth, the heroine of this tale is also a woman, Esther.

The story begins with a drunken seven-day feast hosted by the King of Persia. At the end of the event 'when he was merry with wine' he commands his queen Vashti to come and do a twirl for the assembled male audience and she refuses. This creates a crisis of sorts. Wise men tell the king that he must make an example of her because 'the queen's conduct will come to the ears of all women and embolden them to treat their husbands with disrespect'. So he banishes her and looks for another, to make an example of her. In that way order was restored and every man was once again master in his own house, but he needs a queen. One whole chapter describes the process whereby Esther becomes queen, having been a concubine. She keeps her Jewishness secret but demonstrates her loyalty to the king by denouncing plotters against him.

However, an enmity arises between Esther's father and the prime minister. The latter hatches a plot to kill all the Jews in a horrific act of genocide. Esther uses her influence to frustrate the plot. In the end the prime minister is hanged on the gallows he had intended for his Jewish enemy; Esther's father is promoted and the Jews are spared, going on to slaughter lots of their enemies. People seeing this evidence of God's favour, convert to Judaism in droves, and who can blame them.

The book of **Ecclesiastes** is quite different. This is part of the Wisdom literature, comparable with Proverbs in its style, and containing an anthology of wise observations about the human condition. Chapter 3 is particularly well known for its observation that begins 'For everything there is a season and a time for every purpose under heaven', which is sometimes read in funerals, and which has formed the basis of a popular folk song. The overall theme of this short book is that life is short and there is no guarantee of anything after it, so make the most of it. Its inclusion in the Bible has sometimes been regarded as controversial.

Lamentations is what we might call the war poetry section of the Old Testament. Here we see a series of formal poetic reflections on the fall of Jerusalem prior to the Exile, reflecting on the events that are described in narrative form at 2 Kings 25.8ff., and the scroll is read on the solemn festival that commemorates those events. In the Hebrew scriptures this book is called 'How?' and that is quite a good summary of its contents. The book questions how this could have happened, how God could have allowed it to happen, and asks, effectively, how can we continue to believe in God as a result of its having happened?

Song of Songs has variously been described as a work of Old Testament pornography, and as a masterpiece of divine sanction for sensual love. It consists of a series of erotic love poems in which we hear from a female, a male, a female chorus and a male chorus. The initiative is taken by the female voice and there have been suggestions of a female author. Traditionally the text has been read as an allegory for the relationship between God and Israel or between Jesus and the Church, but modern scholars often consider this both forced and unnecessary, and believe the contents should be read at face value.

Finally, we might include the books of **Jonah** and **Daniel** in this group. They are both included among the minor prophets in the Bible but do not really belong there. Jonah is a narrative tale about a prophet rather than a series of prophecies. He is sent on a mission to Israel's enemy Nineveh, but tries to evade the responsibility of giving God's word to them. The first part of the book demonstrates that God's will cannot be frustrated in this way, and that his prophetic word of judgement and his offer of forgiveness and a new start cannot be suppressed. The second part shows how difficult it is for the Jewish Jonah to come to terms with the implications of what he has been asked to do.

Daniel, the latest book of the Old Testament, is partly another novel, describing the plight of a good Jewish boy at the mercy of a powerful king in the Babylonian exile, and how his faith in God empowers him to overcome his problems, the best-known of which is his ordeal in the lions' den. It is also partly a series of visions setting out, in poetic form, the aspirations of religious people who want to maintain faith in God in the face of so much evidence of what is wrong in the world, and so of the need for a new world order. These visions gave to religious people of Jesus' generation a vocabulary with which to express their hopes, and with which to understand the significance of Jesus in relation to them. Key terms from this late writing include: Son of Man, parousia and resurrection.

What do we need to know to make sense of this material?

With the exception of Song of Songs, it is useful to locate each of these books in relation to the experience of exile. We have to attempt to imagine, in the first place, just what a trauma this experience was, and not just in the physical sense. It called into question all the landmarks of meaning that had given the people of Israel security and identity for centuries, as the account of the development of Israel in the history books describes it. God had promised this people a special relationship. He had promised them a land and progeny. To someone who had depended piously on this understanding, the Exile represented a massively broken series of promises. Hence it was a crisis for God in popular understanding, even though the Bible presents it as more of a crisis for the people.

In time, various writers, as we have seen, interpret the experience in a more positive way. They either regard it as a sharp lesson from which people needed to learn, so as to avoid disaster in the future. Or, in a more positive way still, they regard it as an opportunity to learn new things about God, and to see their former understanding as naïve and incomplete. Either way, there is no room for an interpretation based on denial that the tragedy has occurred, and that perhaps is the contribution of **Lamentations**. Its description of trauma, bereavement and loss will be recognizably authentic to anyone who has suffered fundamental trauma. It is honest and brutal. It raises openly the questions that need to be asked. It looks in vain for a word from God (Where was God in all this?) and wonders publicly how faith can be restored in a context in which things can never be the same again.

Some took the view that the experience of Exile taught the community of faith new things about God, and particularly about his being the one God. As we have seen in Chapter 7, this has some implications for creation theology, which we can see worked out in the Wisdom literature. The writings with which we are concerned in this chapter raise further issues, though **Ecclesiastes** belongs to the wisdom family of writings and it can be seen as the adolescent and subversive member of it.

If God is the God of all creation, he is surely also the God of all peoples, and it is the implications of that which we see being worked out in the books of **Jonah** and **Ruth**. If God is the God of all nations, then he must be God to them in the same way that he is God to Israel. That means that he must make clear to other nations their responsibilities and hold them to account; but he must also make available to them the offer of forgiveness and grace. Jonah is a description of just how hard this is to accept in practice. It's like suddenly having an adopted sibling enter the family and having to learn the hard way that mum and dad love them just as much as they love you. This does show us the beginnings of a theology of difference, which is absolutely essential once all adherents of the faith stop having other cultural things in common. What this amounts to is that Israel has a special role to be a beacon to the nations, but ironically this special role only makes the hurt more acute. Jonah states the problem without resolving it – which is pretty honest because it still isn't resolved over 2,000 years later.

The book of **Ruth** is a corrective to those who want to live in denial about this new discovery of God's nature and activity, and who want to re-draw old boundaries and have a faith based on racial purity. Ezra chapter 10 gives a pretty good description of that mindset. Ruth not only shows that king David was not racially pure, but it also presents a picture of the kind of values that underlie the Sinai Covenant and on which religious life ought to be based. These include: justice, love, faithfulness, truth, generosity, hospitality and concern for the least. These are 'transferable' qualities that do not depend upon race and are to be found in good people everywhere, even in Moab. It is in beaconing these qualities and the nature of the agreement or covenant that underlies them that the vocation of Israel in the newly recognized realm of God is to be pursued. However, the practical arrangements on the ground are far from that ideal. Jews are persecuted when they settle in foreign places, and live in a state of constant vulnerability. **Esther** is written for that context. Alone among the books of the Bible it does not specifically mention God, but he may be there in code, and certainly his influence is seen as determining the course of events. This might just be a pantomime romp were it not for:

• The seriousness of the genocide which is planned against them.

- The bloody revenge which the Jews take when they gain power.

Daniel is also a persecuted foreigner, but most interest in this book (which is also a creative work of fiction – Daniel means 'God's judgement') derives from the visions at the end of it. Though this is a small section of the Old Testament, it is very important in theological terms, and it too is a development of new theological thinking. If God is the creator of all things then it must follow that he is also the designer of history. That thought helps us with one of our other problems which was: If God was creator, why are there so many things wrong in the world and why is there so much suffering about? Why didn't he make a better job of it? But if God designed history then perhaps he has organized it as a series of ages, and perhaps his aim is to redress the problems of this age in the next one.

Now this is a huge subject to which a book like this can make only passing reference, but in fact a whole stack of works appeared, based on this kind of thinking, which came to be known as apocalyptic writings, of which Daniel is our best Old Testament example. These writings looked forward to a new age, which would be heralded perhaps by a special agent, a Son of Man or a Messiah, accompanied by all kinds of phenomena, including perhaps resurrection or a coming (parousia) on the clouds, in order to establish a new kingdom of God. It was these kinds of terms that the Gospel writers, especially, used to describe the significance of Jesus' ministry, and therein lies their importance.

Song of Songs is an enigmatic book which does not relate to any historic period and is unconnected with any other biblical genre. The allegorical interpretation is probably responsible for its being included in the Bible at all, but if the face-value reading is correct that does at least give us a new insight into the process of inspiration and providence as well as showing us that God has a sense of humour.

How can we use this material?

Perhaps the most obvious use of the **Lamentations** material is the pastoral one. Here is a book for those who have suffered trauma of the kind that casts doubt on all that was once regarded as sure. Those experiences will vary. For some they may be 9/11-type events; for others they may be natural disasters in which they were involved. Some may have actual experiences of exile and some may be coming to terms with historic sufferings, such as slavery, that have a bearing on their present identity. Others may be coming to terms with terminal illness in themselves or others or with bereavement of someone close to them. Lamentations is about fighting denial and giving articulation to pain and grief. It gives permission to ask questions, to be angry, and to accuse God.

Read 📖 *Lamentations 3.1–18, then continue to verse 33. The first part of the reading describes utter desolation. Is there anything here that you can identify with? Can you imagine circumstances in which to articulate grief in this way might be helpful? The second part of the reading contains the book's only ray of hope. What is the effect of this? Does it negate the earlier grief, or represent a further stage in dealing with it?*

Ruth, Jonah and **Esther** might all be useful resources in the question (a very contemporary question) of how we deal with difference. Though they deal with racial and so religious difference, in fact they have application to other kinds of gender and life-style difference as well. In a world in which a clash of religious cultures is regularly announced, these books give us material on which to reflect on the question: Who (if anyone) is my enemy?

Read 📖 *Esther chapter 7. This reads almost like a piece of farce. What do you think is the effect of describing horrific events in this rather light way? How would your attitude differ towards this reading depending on whether you were (a) Jewish, (b) a*

*member of some other minority, (c) someone who could identify
more readily with the majority – with the king and his court?
What does that tell you about the problems of difference and
what contribution do Bible books like this make do you think?*

The book of **Daniel** invites us to consider what is wrong with
the world. Apocalyptic writing generally comes from situations
of oppression and the kind of suffering which is a consequence
of occupation and powerlessness. Through these writings we
are asked to identify with those whose understanding of their
plight is such that no human agency might be imagined to
improve it, and that only the possible intervention of God might
bring hope.

For a typical example read 📖 ***Daniel 8.1–14.*** *Here we see a
coded vision which we can be sure relates to the political
movements of the time and the particular anxieties of the faithful. It ends with a message of reassurance for them. Despite all
appearance to the contrary God will act and all will be well.
Can you think of areas where your faith is at odds with your
experience, and where problems seem so intractable that only
some extraordinary intervention can bring about change? We
sometimes use the term miracle to describe this kind of thing.
Have you ever experienced anything like that? Does thinking
along these lines help to make the book of Daniel a little more
accessible?*

I have sometimes liked to think of **Ecclesiastes** as a letter from
an old man of faith to a grandchild. Do you find any resonance
in the idea of a society in which things are changing rapidly, old
certainties breaking down, and where the young look in vain for
ideals and something or someone to believe in? The author
counters the prevailing view that money and wealth are worthwhile in themselves; counters the prevailing view that injustice
and suffering in this life might be reversed in the next and pro-
motes the view that virtue is its own reward, and God's gift is to
enjoy life.

Read 📖 *Ecclesiastes chapter 9 to get a sense of the style and sentiments of the book. Do you think this is suitable to be read at a Christian funeral? Why do you answer as you do?*

Song of Songs can be read in a more relaxed context. This is, after all, a love story. The way that it is told reminds us of the importance of fantasy in the development of close relationships, and perhaps also offers comfort or reassurance that close and passionate erotic love has divine sanction. Read 📖 *Song of Songs 4.1–12. Do you think this is suitable for inclusion in the Bible? What does your answer tell you about your attitude to the Bible?*

This concludes our introduction to the Old Testament. Other books were written between the second century BCE and the time of Jesus. Some of these are contained in a collection called the Apocrypha, which is included in some Bibles. Others are available in scholarly collections from libraries. These books were not considered holy writ in quite the same sense as the books that did make it into the Bible as we know it. Many are apocalypses like Daniel, but there are other genres as well. At the time of Jesus, the third section, 'Writings', of the Hebrew Bible was still not fixed, so these works were circulating in learned (and sometimes not so learned) circles in his day. A whole new family of religious writings was about to hit the streets though. In time that too would be the subject of consideration and discernment by the religious establishment. There would be a further process of sifting and collecting. And that would give us what we now recognize as the New Testament.

9

Getting Started on Gospels

What's included?

Gospels are (probably) a Christian invention. The word 'gospel' means 'good news' and relates to a genre of writing only found in the Christian Church and which cannot be described adequately in any other way. In the New Testament there are four Gospels. Three of them, **Matthew**, **Mark** and **Luke**, clearly enjoy some kind of literary relationship. That is to say, they are like each other in their style, in the order in which they include material, and they even have substantial verbal similarities. It is possible indeed to set up a kind of synopsis, so-called, of these three Gospels, placing them in three columns side by side in order to look at them together to see just how similar they are. For that reason they are called 'Synoptic Gospels'. The fourth Gospel, **John**, is different in many respects from the other three. It has different vocabulary, a different style and ethos, and a different order of events. It omits much of what the Synoptic Gospels include and includes material that they do not. Like the rest of the New Testament these works are written not in Hebrew but in Greek.

At first sight, these writings look like simple eyewitness accounts of the ministry of Jesus, with a few pieces of interpretation thrown in. They appear to contain quoted sayings of Jesus, together with stories that he told, called parables, woven into a narrative account of his activity including: how he got started, what he thought he was doing, who he thought he was, the people he called to join him, and how they all got on together. There are stories of healing, stories of Jesus demonstrating various kinds of power (over the elements or even over mental illness), of his addressing crowds of people, and accounts of his clashes with different representatives of authority. There's quite a lot about the circumstances surrounding his death and the effect it had. Around 200 years ago, this kind of face-value literal reading was commonplace, but since then scholars have made a journey of discovery, which has encouraged us to see the Gospels as sophisticated and multi-layered pieces of writing that actually take quite a lot of unravelling.

What do we need to know to make sense of this material?

The first thing we need to do is pay close attention to the text and note the intriguing problem it raises.

Reflection

There's really only one way to appreciate the Gospels, and that's to read them from beginning to end, one at a time. Begin with Mark. Then read Matthew, and try to write down what seems different about

- *the style*
- *the content*
- *the atmosphere of the writing*
- *the kind of audience it might appeal to.*

Finally, read Luke. Now using two columns write down first, the things that Matthew and Luke seem to have in common, that differ from Mark; and then the things that make them different from each other. This may well take you quite a while, but it will help to highlight some of the things that scholars have been fascinated by for the last couple of centuries.

If you don't have that much time but just want to see an example of the problem, read Matthew 9.9–13, Mark 2.13–17 and Luke 5.27–32.

The first things we probably notice are these.

- Mark is the shortest Gospel.
- Matthew and Luke both contain some stories, such as the temptation of Jesus in Matthew chapter 4 and Luke chapter 4, which do not appear in Mark.
- Both Matthew and Luke each contain stories that do not appear elsewhere, such as the parable of the sheep and the goats in Matthew chapter 25, or the parable of the Good Samaritan in Luke chapter 10.
- There are remarkable verbal similarities, but sometimes differences in detail between the Gospels.

These Gospels do not read like biographies. They deal with very selective parts of Jesus' life in a very disproportionate way. Half the material describes just one week in his life, while 27 years are almost entirely missing. Biographies also tend to have more overt comment from the author. So what are we to make of all this?

Imagining the story

Some scholars have tried to imagine the history of the process that led to the Gospels as we know them, and their most commonly accepted conclusions would give us the following story.

We assume that Jesus' crucifixion took place around 29 CE, and that his followers considered the events of the first Easter as incredibly significant. Stories about Jesus were circulating by word of mouth in lots of different ways. Some of them came from the disciples' eyewitness accounts; some came from the stories collected in particular localities; some were popular with particular groups of people. As the earliest Christian community grew, these stories fed its worship, reflection and teaching, and in the process, took on a shape and character of their own.

Some became part of the Church's rhetoric, being adapted to argue the case for Christianity against its detractors. Some became part of the Church's liturgy. Others were put to use as illustrations in early sermons. Embellishments and stylistic additions meant that the original 'raw data' soon became indistinguishable from the new material in which it was presented. Over time, similar material might have formed the basis of informal collections, either oral or written down. Eventually, over 30 years and at least a whole generation later, the author of Mark gathered enough material together to form a two-part document. One half of it described Jesus' last week, leading up to his crucifixion – the so-called passion narrative – and the other was a kind of introduction to help set a context for that, and a means of interpreting it. This Gospel is used by Mark's associates and church community, but also gains wider circulation. (Incidentally, we're not sure who 'Mark' was, but in this story it really doesn't matter). It's actually Mark who invents the genre 'Gospel' by opening his work with the words: 'The beginning of the gospel of Jesus Christ, the Son of God.'

This piece of work comes into the possession of the author of Matthew's Gospel. His community lives in a different place, and is made up of people who are different from Mark's community. They probably had different nationality and a different cultural background, and they are facing different questions: questions that Mark does not apparently address. This author also has access to material that Mark does not have. So the Gospel of Matthew appears. And in due course, and in like fashion, Luke also emerges. Each Gospel was written for a purpose, for a specific audience, and perhaps in relation to specific problems and controversies that were affecting particular Christian communities.

Placing the Gospels

More recently, scholars have moved away from viewing the Gospels just in a historical frame, and instead of asking how they developed to reach their present form, or what were the communities like for which they wrote, they have concentrated on the text as we have it, as a piece of literature. And so they have asked more questions about the techniques the authors used to present their case and tell their story. There's been a renewed interest in how plots develop and how characters are drawn.

So when we read the Gospels, what are we looking for, what are they meant to tell us? The likelihood is that each of the authors wants their Gospel to tell us something about:

- How we are to understand the ministry of Jesus and in what cultural terms we can describe its significance.
- How we can assess the legitimate character of the community of Christians.
- The distinctiveness of this new religion.

In the process they want their Gospels to shed light on wider questions of belief and human existence such as:

- What is the destiny of the world and its people, and does life have meaning and purpose?
- What is the function of suffering in human experience?
- Is it inevitable that human evil is stronger than the powers of goodness, or can humankind somehow be changed or redeemed?
- How should humans behave?

The Gospels also tell us some things inadvertently, such as:

- The kind of problems of belief that affected different communities at different times and in different areas.
- How different writers tried to communicate what they had received by translating it into the language and ideas that their hearers would understand, in other words, how religious communication might function.
- The kind of controversies and adversaries that called for robust arguments: What were the local and immediate issues?

What the Gospels are *not* meant, by their authors, to be are:

- A historic and dispassionate archive account of the life of a famous man.
- A record for posterity of what really happened.
- An A–Z account for enquirers about Christianity.

Accessing the culture

One of the things that gives the Gospels their particular character, but at the same time can make them difficult to access, is the fact that they are written from a culture far removed from our own. The only ways available to the writers to describe the problems outlined above, and to describe the significance of Jesus in relation to them, are those provided by the ongoing story of God and the Jewish people that we encountered in the Old Testament. We have to try to put ourselves in the position of a people who are expecting their God to intervene in human history to make right a lot of things that have gone wrong. What religious people (and perhaps that's a description which extends to a much wider populace than it might today) were hoping for, was the kind of intervention that would transform society, transform individuals and even open up a completely new era in history by transforming creation itself.

The way in which these hopes were expressed has shaped the vocabulary and style of the Gospels in particular. When thinking about a new kind of community, pre-New Testament people spoke of a new rule or kingdom of God, with a new king like David (which is what the term 'Son of David' means in Hebrew). In this kingdom, old values would be transformed and a whole new set of values take their place to bring about greater justice. In thinking about how this might happen, there was an expectation that a special agent of God – perhaps a new 'anointed one' like David (the Hebrew term is messiah, which translates into Greek as *christos*) – or a new 'representative human' (or, to use another Hebrew idiom, Son of Man) would be the catalyst that would usher in the new era.

This figure would have an important role for those who had kept faithful to their religion through times of persecution and doubt. He would present them to God for vindication. Pictures of this include a 'coming' (Greek: *parousia*) to God on the clouds of heaven. One of the ways in which individuals would be transformed was through a new offer of forgiveness. All of this would pave the way for a new age to dawn, the 'age to come', when evil would be overcome and all that God had intended in creation, but which human agency had corrupted, would be restored. The recognizable event that would signal the beginning of this new age would be the almost unimaginable prospect of the resurrection of the dead, with the messiah figure leading the way. It is only when we can recognize the hopes and questions that lie behind this series of expectations, expressed in this way, that we can see the urgency of the Gospel writers, and see why they thought the good news was good.

Who is Jesus for us?

But this also highlights the difficulty we have in 'translating' this good news into terms that make any sense in today's world. The key questions for the Gospel characters were not about whether God existed. They were about whether or not Jesus was 'the one who is to come', and whether that meant that the new age was about to dawn. And the cutting edge of the whole Gospel message is that Christians believed that Jesus was in fact that very one, even though he did not tick the boxes for the religious people of the time, in that:

- He did not keep himself pure but mixed with outcasts and sinners.
- He criticized the very religious people who were expecting him to congratulate them, and even accused them of mis-representing God.
- He did not arrive in a great supernatural flourish or live in splendour.
- Worst of all, he suffered and died.

The task of the Gospel writers is to persuade people that despite all this, Jesus was in fact the 'one who is to come' and that in some sense his death does usher in, through the resurrection, the dawn of a new age, with the possibility of a new community (what we have come to think of as the Church) made new by the offer of forgiveness. In other words, the Gospel writers are saying that the religious community of the time had somehow got it wrong about God, and that Jesus' life and death tells them (and us) a whole lot of new things about God that they (and we) hadn't realized before.

What's special about Mark?

Each of the Gospels is special in two ways. First, each has a particular literary character that makes its way of presenting material different from the others. But also each has what we might call a theological character. That is, it is concerned with different aspects of the story about God and its implications, and has a particular 'take' on them.

Among the literary characteristics are these.

Mark's favourite way of describing a situation is to use the same technique that stand-up comics use. (This man goes into a pub and he goes up to the bar and he says . . .). It's called the historic present and is easy to recognize in the original Greek. This gives a sense of movement and immediacy. It's also very simple and lends itself to being repeated by word of mouth. Other techniques, which contribute to the same effect, are using the word 'and' continuously (in chapter 3, 29 verses begin with the word); using the word 'immediately' (41 times in all) and using the word 'again' (25 times in all).

He likes using what are called diminutives. In other words, instead of saying 'child' he says 'kiddie'. This too reflects an oral story-telling background.

His account contains lots of vivid detail that Matthew and Luke omit. Examples can be found at 4.37 (mention of a cushion), 6.40 (at the feeding the people are seated 'as in flower beds'), 8.24 (vivid description of what the blind man can see), and 10.16 (he takes the children 'in the crook of his arm'). These examples are not always apparent in translation.

He quotes verbatim from other languages. Examples are 6.27, 12.14 and 15.39 (from Latin) and 3.17, 7.11, 14.36 (from Aramaic).

When it comes to a special character in terms of ideas, Mark is very interested in who Jesus was, and why he had to die, which after all is a huge scandal. To claim that someone is God, and that at the same time he suffered and died, is for most people, then and now, a contradiction in terms.

Mark's portrayal of Jesus is of someone who is emotional and passionate, a man among men. He is deeply caring and concentrates on healing, giving it a wider significance and connecting it with 'saving'. In this caring role he presents a model to the new Christian community, to define what the religious task actually is.

There is a deep interest in suffering. This stems from the questions about why Jesus had to suffer if he really were God, but may also have a resonance with the community addressed in that they may themselves have been called upon to suffer persecution or even martyrdom.

The most frequent description of Jesus in this Gospel is as 'teacher', and it has been pointed out that 40 per cent of the verses have teaching content, but the content of the teaching is not revealed as fully as in the other Gospels.

There is a strong international theme in this Gospel. (Many scholars think it was written for a congregation in Rome.) It concentrates attention in Galilee, the most cosmopolitan area of Israel, rather than Jerusalem, and has a particular interest in the mission to non-Jews.

The most common designation of Jesus is 'Son of God', which is far more common in Greek religion than in the Old Testament. The term 'Son of Man' (whose most famous Old Testament appearance is Daniel 7.13) is also used and, interestingly, this is the only designation that we find on Jesus' own lips – this is how he is made to describe himself.

And yet ironically, in this Gospel, Jesus seems to go to a lot of trouble to conceal who he really is. He's always telling his disciples to keep quiet about it, but his attempts fail. There's a lot of debate about what the author intended by this device.

How can we use this material?

We might begin by asking the same question as Mark: who is Jesus for us, and in what way can we describe him? **Read** 📖 **Mark chapter 5.** *What in these stories is hard to access and what is easy? We see here a picture of a Jesus who is both powerful and compassionate with discernment about the personal effects of suffering on families and communities. On the other hand, we see a very quaint description of mental illness, and some supernatural descriptions of cure. Nowadays we have access to many portrayals of Jesus in film and television. If you were a film director, how would you 'shoot' chapter 5 in a way that conveyed both the significance of Jesus, and offered him as a model for behaviour and attitude?*

In chapter 1 Mark presents Jesus as saying, 'the time has arrived, the kingdom of God is upon you'. Then we hardly hear anything about the kingdom again until the beginning of chapter 9. The implication is that what Jesus does is a demonstration of what the kingdom is like. Look through those chapters again and see if they strike you as being at odds with current culture. In what way do these accounts show that God's rule is so very different from the values of our own society? If you were to imagine these scenes somehow transposed into our time, what demonstrations could Jesus make of the alternative kingdom of God that would be most decisive for you? What would he have to do to persuade you?

Read 📖 **Mark 8.37—9.13.** *This contains two of the summons to secrecy. Both of them are about the significance of Jesus. There is also a reference to the widely held belief that Elijah would somehow herald the appearance of the one who was to* *come. (Some early Christians clearly saw John the Baptist in this way.) The bottom line of all this is the question of just how evident Jesus' status was. Was it only really possible to piece the story together in reflective afterthought? You might think about how the really significant insights into your own life were received. Was it blindingly obvious that something was the case or only after other interpretative experiences and tools were in place? Does this way of thinking give you further insight into the writing of a passage like this?*

Read 📖 Mark chapter 16. Depending on the Bible you choose, you will probably find a most confusing set of alternative endings set out. It is very likely that the account actually ends at verse 8. If this is so, what do verses 9–19 tell you about how subsequent generations misunderstood what Mark was trying to say about resurrection?

The Gospels give us our first insight into the upheaval in religious thinking that was caused both by Jesus' ministry and especially by his crucifixion, and the first attempts to relate that to what was already (thought to be) known about God. The Gospel of Mark sets the template, which both Matthew and Luke adopt.

10

Getting Started on Matthew and Luke

What's included?

Matthew and Luke, along with Mark, are Synoptic Gospels (see the last chapter). The authors of Matthew and Luke appear to have had access to Mark and used it as a source. Each of them has used most of Mark and followed his order. Each has made substantial additions, some of which they share, some of which they do not. The material in the 'what do we need to know?' section of the last chapter is equally applicable to this. Like Mark, each of these Gospels has its own literary character and its own theological concerns. Each was presumably produced for a subtly different purpose. That is hinted at in the authors' own descriptions. Whereas Mark is called a Gospel, Matthew is described as a 'Book' (the first word of 1.1, not always obvious in English translation) and Luke as an 'orderly account' (1.3).

What's special about Matthew?

Matthew and Jewishness

If you read Matthew trying to find clues as to the kind of audience it was meant for, the first thing that might strike you is that this is a very tense Gospel with lots of argument, and a strong sense of crisis. From this we might conclude that the audience was a Christian community in conflict. In itself this is not strange. Conflict is often a catalyst for Christian writing. Most of the New Testament would not have been written had there not been conflict, and often between Christians. In the case of Matthew, the conflict seems to be with Jews. The writer is obviously very familiar with Jewish ways of writing, and may have been a converted Jew, as may his congregation. There is some discussion among experts as to whether these Christians still went to the synagogue or not, and whether the heat generated is because the new Christians are regarded as traitors by their former comrades, or whether the Christians are themselves offended by their former comrades' refusal to acknowledge Jesus as the one who was to come. There were great similarities between the Christians and the Jews, and that is often a situation that prompts fierce rhetoric as neither side wants to be confused with the other. The New Testament does little justice to the Pharisees, in particular, who get a very bad press, probably precisely because they are so similar to Christians rather than the reverse.

Jewish written works are often divided into five sections. This is true of the book of Psalms, for example, but especially true of the first section of the Hebrew Bible, the Torah or Law, which contains five books. One notable literary feature of Matthew is that it, too, appears to have a fivefold structure. Five times in the Gospel we find a large block of teaching material concluding with the words 'and when Jesus finished . . .' (7.28, 11.1, 13.53, 19.1 and 26.1). Some scholars have said that this is a conscious attempt to present, in a stylized form, a new law. They have pointed to the way in which Jesus is presented in Matthew as a second Moses, wonderfully saved from infant massacre, then standing on a mountain to speak about God's law. Others have considered these five collections to be more of a teaching mechanism, gathering material of the same type together into little manuals, each with its own theme. If we followed this scheme, then we would say the first is about the law (the so-called sermon on the mount), the second about mission, the third is about the kingdom of God, the fourth about church discipline and the final section is about the end of the age. These sections are among the best known and most often quoted parts of the Gospel.

However, it must be said that there are lots of verbal repetitions in the Gospel, which may or may not be deliberate and may or may not aid our understanding. For example, 4.17 and 16.21 both include the phrase, 'then Jesus began'. Or again, 4.23 and 9.35 seem to bracket one section that describes Jesus' ministry of teaching and healing.

One particular and noticeable feature is the way Matthew quotes the Old Testament. There are several examples in chapter 2, usually including a variation of the phrase: 'This happened to fulfil what the prophet said.' There are 12 such quotations in the Gospel as a whole and at least 10 of them have been 'adapted to fit', in a way which would appal modern writers. 1.22 and 23 is a well-known example. Here the author is quoting Isaiah 7.14, but there is a problem. In Hebrew there are two words for 'virgin'. One has the technical sense with which we associate the word today and which is usually intended when we speak of the 'virgin birth'. The other simply means young woman of marriageable age – something like the old English word 'damsel'. It is the latter of these that the Hebrew of Isaiah intends, but from the Greek, Matthew uses this text as a proof of the former point. In other words, what he's using as a proof text, isn't proof at all.

Difficult to access?

This is just one feature of the Gospel that is said to make it the most inaccessible to the modern reader. There are other reasons why this modern reader might find it difficult to identify with or be gripped or persuaded by this Gospel. They include:

- The emphasis on crisis, and having to make a choice now! This is very much tied up with descriptions of the end of the age that are often lurid and fantastic. They are part of the family of apocalyptic writings which we met in the book of Daniel, and have to be unpacked very fully before we can appreciate them.
- In turn, and also a feature of apocalyptic, there is an empha-

sis on reward and punishment. The descriptions of punishment sit uneasily to the modern mind with descriptions of a gentle loving Jesus. The questions about reward are of a different kind – challenging the morality of actions that are carried out in the hope of reward.

- The claims that are made on followers to be perfect and to be wholly committed or risk punishment are not exactly attractive.
- There is little sympathy in the Gospel for those who are trying hard to live a good life and relying on their religious traditions for legitimacy.

I like to think of Matthew as a young person's Gospel. It is full of idealism, and it presents its truths in a very black and white, take it or leave it kind of way that leaves no room for compromise. The crisis is now, you must decide now, and it's full commitment or nothing. If you think of it as coming from a very tense situation and if you accept that the apocalyptic backdrop is a cultural set of clothes that would have meant different things to the audience, from what they mean to us, then it is possible to read this Gospel to advantage. And there are some important themes to emerge.

Matthew's agenda

Matthew is very strong on accountability. What he is saying is that the religious community cannot be smug and complacent. They cannot behave as if God had somehow chosen them for special treatment come what may, and however they behave. They cannot act as if they've got God taped; as if he's so bound by his own rules that they can always know what his next move will be, and that it will always be in their favour. There are a number of ways in which this is expressed.

- People are told that they cannot rely on being part of a particular religious tradition to be right with God, or to be 'saved' (3.9 is a warning to those who want to claim protection through Jewish descent; 7.22 warns that it's not enough to be able to recite the service or even hold some religious office).

- Personal judgement is emphasized and heightened, as we have seen.
- Positive examples of how people and societies should act are provided. Matthew 25.31ff. is a famous story that only occurs in this Gospel, making it clear that people will be judged on how they respond to the least-regarded people – people without food, drink or shelter, for example.

Allied with this perhaps is Matthew's interest in the law. For him this is not an insurance policy, a dead letter, or a lawyer's dream but rather something dynamic and challenging to each new generation. Jesus' own teaching on the law in chapters 5—7 is radical, and gives hints of how laws had been adapted to fit religious comfort zones.

Matthew, like the other Gospel writers, has to 'package' Jesus in a way that will appeal to, help and challenge his hearers. He also uses the terms Son of God and Son of Man. He uses Son of David far more than the others as he explores the relationship between Jewish heritage and Christian radical thinking. He is the only Gospel writer apparently to try to suggest that Jesus is standing in the tradition of Moses (Luke goes out of his way to say that when Jesus addressed the crowds, he did not go up a mountain (Luke 6.17)).

One other characteristic of this Gospel is its interest in the Church. Matthew alone uses the Greek word *ecclesia*, from which we derive English words like ecclesiastical (18.18, 19.10–12). One whole block of his five teaching blocks deals with what you might call 'church matters' and there is a prominence given to Peter that has led to his being accorded special status in some Christian traditions. Some passages have a liturgical ring – that is to say, they sound as if they might have been used in church services. The Lord's Prayer in Matthew (Matthew 6.9ff.), which is different from Luke (Luke 11.2ff.), might be one example. Also the ending of the Gospel in chapter

28 verses 19 to 20 gives instructions to the disciples in a very churchy-sounding way, including the formula 'in the name of the Father and of the Son and of the Holy Spirit', which is commonplace in church services today.

What's special about Luke?

To move from Matthew to Luke is like moving from youth to middle age. The style is more considered and literary. Luke addresses his readers, not so much from the middle of a conflict, but as an observer, considering several sources in order to provide a reliable and coherent account. All of this is evident from the first four verses of the Gospel. As we proceed further we sense a different mood from that in Matthew's Gospel. Although the Gospel certainly does not lack 'edge' and challenge, the reader is not made to feel that s/he is in the midst of a crisis. The long view that Luke achieves makes his Gospel seem more like history writing, though everything we have said about the Gospel genre remains true here. This was also a piece of work written for a specific purpose, and addressing specific concerns, and it has its own characteristics. It is also worth pointing out that scholars believe, almost universally, that Luke is part 1 of a two-part series, part 2 being the New Testament book, The Acts of the Apostles. Part 1, the Gospel, is longer than the other Synoptic Gospels. Between one third and one quarter of all Gospel material is found in Luke alone.

A universal Gospel

The most immediately apparent characteristic of the Gospel is that whereas Matthew, for the most part, has a particular interest in Jewish culture and destiny, Luke appears to have a more universal interest.

- Luke 3.23–38 includes a genealogy of Jesus that goes back to Adam, and so to God. The equivalent in Matthew (1.1–17) only goes back to Abraham. This suggests that for Matthew's readers, the context in which we have to place Jesus is the history of Israel; whereas for Luke's readers, the context in which we have to place him is the history of humankind, or even the history of creation.

- Only Luke includes Samaritans in the narrative in a positive way. At 17.11–19, it is the Samaritan leper who returns to give thanks. At 10.30–37, it is the Samaritan who goes to the aid of the man who has been mugged, after representatives of the Jewish establishment have passed by.
- Luke sets out salvation as something that is available to other 'outsiders' as well. This point is well made in the story of Zacchaeus, which only occurs in this Gospel (19.1–10).
- Luke appears better disposed towards Gentiles (non-Jews) than Matthew. He misses out verses from Matthew that might offend them (e.g. Matthew 7.6) and, in his own context-setting introduction makes special mention of the Gentiles (2.32).
- Luke is also particularly inclusive of the poor and despised. The woman of the streets in 7.36ff. is presented very sympathetically, and a whole chapter (chapter 15) is devoted to the importance of 'the lost'. That chapter is introduced with reports about how Jesus was being criticized for being so inclusive.
- Luke 1.68–79, referred to in some churches as the Magnificat, is a stirring call to social revolution that will see the lowly lifted up and the high and mighty brought down.
- Having said that, Luke also appears to understand the mind-set of the rich, and to be unwilling to abandon them utterly (see Luke 12.15ff., for example).
- Luke gives women a greater status and role in his Gospel than do the other Synoptic Gospel writers. Mary has more importance in this Gospel than elsewhere.

So the challenge in Luke's Gospel does not appear to be whether you meet the criteria for belonging or not, so much as the challenge of inclusivity, and of recognizing the universal claims and interests of God.

History

The second main characteristic of the Gospel is its interest in history. Luke is keen to relate the events of Jesus' ministry to political history and 'realtime'. He alone places the birth of Jesus in relation to the census ordered by the Roman authorities, and he alone makes the case for the political innocence of Jesus, as he tells the story of his trial and death. The conclusion he appears to want the reader to draw is that the political establishment has nothing to fear from Jesus. On the other hand, no other Gospel writer is as anxious to highlight the significance of Jesus in the whole canvas of human history. Some people have suggested that the Gospel is so arranged as to present the ministry and time of Jesus as the benchmark of significance in the history of the world, by which all other events are judged. In comparison with Matthew, Luke plays down any return of Jesus as judge. He describes a Church (as we shall see in Acts) that is dug in for the long haul, and the task of converting the whole world, rather than one that sees itself as a short-term community awaiting some further event.

The Holy Spirit

Thirdly, it is in this Gospel (and also in Acts), that we see most mention in the Gospels of the Holy Spirit. For Christians, God is understood in three ways (the so-called doctrine of the Trinity). He is known as Father, creator; he is known as Son, in the person of Jesus and what he did; and he is known as Holy Spirit, the capacity of God to bring life and energy to creation and communities. Each New Testament writer who uses the term Holy Spirit, does so in a slightly different way, but all would recognize that description. The term appears five times in Matthew and four in Mark. In Luke and Acts it appears 53 times.

Just as with Matthew, so with Luke, some detective work can give us clues as to what were the main issues for the Christian community he was addressing. His alternative approach to any imminent return of Jesus suggests that as a possible issue. Some people have seen emphases that suggest he is aware of particular kinds of false or heretical teaching (from groups such as those we know as Gnostics who played down the human side of Jesus in favour of his divine status). The issue of why Jesus had to suffer is still central. Luke does address the question: Who are the real people of God, and how important is mission to the Gentiles?

Luke uses a wider vocabulary and series of ideas to describe or 'package' Jesus. 'Christ' and 'Lord' are his favourite titles, the latter being more accessible to a non-Jewish audience. His is the only Synoptic Gospel to use 'Saviour', another more universal title. Only the disciples call Jesus 'Master' and only his enemies call him 'Rabbi' or 'Teacher'. Luke uses the Old Testament in a different way from Matthew but still regards it as an important means of interpretation. One particularly interesting Old Testament theme that he picks up is the idea of Jesus as servant as well as son (the Greek word used can mean either).

Luke's political and social agenda is a matter of debate. Is the author trying to defend Jesus to the state, or is he trying to defend the state to the Christian community? Was Jesus actually as much of a threat to social order as his Magnificat introduction and his 'first sermon' in Luke 4.16ff. suggest? Is his portrayal of women favourable or not? What are we to make of passages such as Luke 10.38ff.?

How can we use this material?

Christians use the Gospels in a whole host of ways. Although there is no hierarchy of status within the Bible, in practice it is the Gospels that are considered the real foundation documents for the faithful. Many churches ensure that whatever else is read from the Bible, each major service includes a reading from the Gospels, and sometimes a special posture (such as standing up) is adopted to emphasize its special authority. Other New Testament writers also appear to accept that 'words of the Lord' have a special authority and importance.

Hence Christians refer to these documents:

- to seek to know the will of God
- to determine the appropriate kinds of religious and social organization to bring about what God desires
- to understand themselves, the human condition and the way they relate with others
- to interpret world events
- to understand better how to communicate with God through prayer and worship.

They have the advantage that you can read almost any chapter at random, and can make sense of it as an incident in the life and ministry of Jesus.

To get more out of Gospel reading, there are a number of things we can do.

One is to compare how different Gospel writers use the same or similar material.

Read 📖 Mark 4.35–41 and then, Matthew 8.23–27. These two accounts look very similar at first sight. But actually they have substantial differences. Mark uses the language that a weatherman might use to describe the storm. Attention is focused on just how laid-back Jesus is about the whole affair in order to highlight his power. The language the disciples use to speak to him is 'rough' language of panic. When the storm has subsided he admonishes the disciples. This is essentially a private affair between him and them. Matthew, on the other hand, places the story in a context of discussion about what it means to be a follower. He uses the word 'earthquake' to describe the storm – the same word used in chapter 28 to describe Jesus' appearance to the disciples after the resurrection. Their address to him sounds more like a prayer (Lord, save us) than a panicky shout from the terrified. He admonishes them while the storm is still raging, which let's face it, is quite unrealistic, and in this Gospel the whole thing is public. It is the people who ask the questions at the end. One possible interpretation is that while Mark is setting out a demonstration of Jesus' power, Matthew is trying in a more coded way to say something about a church community that is losing heart. If that were true, look again at the Matthew passage. What do you think it might be trying to say? Do you think the message has any relevance for today?

Another is to appreciate the literary skill of the author in a way that points us towards his special intentions and interests.
   Read 📖 ***Luke 15.11–end.*** *See how the author paints the picture of the second son. Do you feel sympathy for him? And yet surely his is the obvious and understandable response. What is the author up to here, do you think?*

Both of these approaches help us to recognize that the Gospels are directed to real religious communities, and that gives those who are members of such communities today opportunity to see if there are issues and problems in common.

Every generation of Christians needs to know who Jesus is for them. Every generation needs to be convinced afresh of what the Church is for. That, in turn, leads to questions about the most appropriate relationship between Church and state, and the extent to which the Church should be involved in political issues. And every human being has questions about the human condition: about creation and death, suffering and evil. These are questions that are dealt with in a different way in subsequent New Testament books.

II

Getting Started on John

To read a chapter on the Gospel of John in an introduction to the Bible is a bit like reading a chapter on *Hamlet* in an introduction to Shakespeare. An instinctive guess would say that there have probably been more commentaries written on this book than on any other in the New Testament. It is a book on which everyone seems to have an opinion, and which you either love or loathe. The amount of interpretative writing it has generated bears witness to the enigmatic quality of the Gospel. Here we leave the relatively straightforward narrative style of the Synoptic Gospels and enter a world of poetry and symbolism, where we suspect that everything we read has a deeper meaning, and that the whole thing is designed to both create, and give an insight into, a world of mystery.

What's special about John?

A favourite starting point for commentators is to speculate about the relationship between John and the other Gospels. Did any of the Synoptics have sight of John? Is John a mature reflection on themes in the Synoptics familiar to him? Do they have separate sources? Which was written first? And so on. The details of that debate are perhaps not too important to us, and there is no real consensus (although currently there is a majority view that John was produced independently of the other Gospels), but what might be more interesting is to note the material that John has in common with the others, and that which is peculiar to his Gospel. The material common to the Synoptics and John includes:

- Ministry of John the Baptist.
- Jesus calling disciples.
- Jesus feeding the five thousand.
- Jesus entering Jerusalem on a donkey.
- Jesus cleansing the temple.
- The last supper.

However, the treatment of each of these topics is significantly different. John's testimony to Jesus, for example, is far more explicit: 'Behold the Lamb of God who takes away the sin of the world!' Also we have no description in this Gospel of Jesus actually being baptized by John. Peter and Andrew are called first as disciples, but in Judea and not Galilee. The cleansing of the temple comes right at the beginning of Jesus' ministry rather than at the end, after the entry into Jerusalem for the last time. The timing of the last supper in relation to the Passover feast, and hence its symbolic significance, are different in John; and the feeding of the five thousand is not part of a Galilean ministry, to be followed by a single journey to Jerusalem. In John Jesus moves back and forth to Jerusalem frequently, his visits timed to coincide with important feasts. (That is if we are to read this as a historic narrative rather than a literary reflection on theological themes.)

Material that is fairly familiar and only appears in John includes:

- The enigmatic opening poem ('In the beginning was the word . . .').
- Changing water into wine at the wedding in Cana.
- The raising of Lazarus from the dead.
- The washing of the disciples' feet at the last supper.
- Jesus appearing to his disciples by the lakeside after the resurrection.

Readers of the Synoptic Gospels will have become familiar with the basic message of the kingdom of God, with Jesus teaching in parables, and with his performing miracles. None of this is to be found in John. The aspiration of Christians is not for the kingdom of God but rather for 'eternal life'. (The Greek phrase here signifies a quality of life, not its length.) There are no parables at all in John. When Jesus speaks, he normally uses the medium of a discourse – and these discourses can be quite long, dense, repetitive and puzzling. Jesus does not perform miracles but he does perform 'signs'. Each of these signs is carefully numbered, and the progression is considered important. There are seven of these altogether and they are:

- The wedding at Cana where Jesus turned water into wine (2.1–11).
- A healing, also at Cana, of the son of a royal officer (4.43–54).
- The healing of the cripple at Bethesda (5.1–14).
- Feeding of the five thousand (6.1–14).
- Walking on water (6.16–21).
- Healing a blind man (9.1–12).
- Raising of Lazarus (11.1–43).

They read differently from the Synoptic miracles. They are usually quite involved stories. Indeed, the discourse material surrounding these signs sometimes appears more important than the sign itself. Their climax is sometimes a saying of Jesus that begins with the words, 'I am . . .'. Altogether there are seven such sayings. They are:

- I am the bread of life (6.35).
- I am the light of the world (8.12).
- I am the door of the sheepfold (10.7).
- I am the good shepherd (10.11).
- I am the resurrection and the life (11.25).
- I am the way the truth and the life (14.6).
- I am the true vine (15.1).

It is likely that if you have heard anything from John's Gospel, it will include at least one of these sayings. The significance of this form is likely to lie in the fact that the Greek for 'I am' corresponds to the Greek version of Exodus 3.14, where God reveals his name to Moses as 'I am'. In other words, this is a pretty heavy clue as to the identity of Jesus.

The signs often invite controversy, as opposed to, say, the miracles in Mark, which inspire awe and confirm authority. Also their style is different. These are 'clumsy' and mechanical compared with their Synoptic counterparts – more like the work of a magician than a divine figure, though Jesus never performs an exorcism in this Gospel. Chapters 2—12 are sometimes referred to as 'The Book of Signs', since there does seem to be an explicit structure based on the progression of the signs. Jesus' pre-passion ministry is fashioned around them. The other structural device that we find in these chapters, and which in a sense continues into the passion narrative, is the way in which the author deals with Jesus' attendance at Jewish festivals.

John, Jesus and the Jews

There is something rather contrived about the way Jesus moves between Galilee and Jerusalem, and the suspicion of something created rather than reported is heightened by the way the narrative signals particular parts of the festival. Chapter 7 is a good place to get a sense of this. These festivals have a symbolism and a history of development of their own. A primitive harvest festival probably used the image of light (for early morning picking of the crop), water (for washing the crop) and grapes (the actual crop). In time these images were in all likelihood re-applied to giver them a meaning related to the Passover and Exodus tradition. What was once a simple harvest ceremony now came to symbolize, in addition, the early morning flight from Egypt. The water may have reminded people of the sustenance provided in the desert, and the grapes, of the promised land. In these passages in John's Gospel we see a further re-application of these ancient traditions. Jesus is the light of the world. Jesus is the living water. Jesus is the true vine. The effect is to say something about the relationship between Jesus and his own Jewish tradition, and something about the relationship between Christianity and Judaism. Most obviously that would be: Jesus and Christianity have superseded Judaism.

The answer to the question: What is the fourth Gospel's attitude to Judaism? is not, however, as straightforward as that. Apparently, in the author we have someone who appears to be steeped in Jewish culture, familiar with the landscape of Jerusalem and Palestine, aware even of details of Jewish domestic practice. And yet when Jews appear in the narrative (and they are usually referred to simply as 'the Jews') it is usually in confrontational situations, where they are treated as enemies. A long-standing explanation for this is that the Gospel was written at a time, late in the first century, when Christians were being expelled from synagogues (as at 9.22). More recent writers have proposed more complicated scenarios.

Passion and reflection

The passion narrative is much longer in John than in any other Gospel, stretching from chapter 13 to chapter 20. In place of the agony in the Garden of Gethsemane we have a four chapter long series of 'mystical' reflections on the traditional basic questions of Christian theology: namely the relationship between the Father, the Son and the Holy Spirit. This reaches a climax in chapter 17 in a prayer, sometimes called the high priestly prayer, in which the relationship between God and believers is set out. At the last supper there are no words spoken over the bread and wine. Instead we have the foot washing incident. When Jesus is arrested, Jesus asks the arresting officer whom he seeks. He replies, 'Jesus of Nazareth'. Jesus replies, three times in all 'I am (he)', echoing once again the formula that once identified the God of the Old Testament. When Jesus is actually hanging on the cross, like Luke but unlike Matthew and Mark, John has him speak a number of significant sayings. All of them are positive. There is no God-forsaken cry in John. His dying cry is one of victory, 'It is finished!' A final chapter has Jesus appear to his disciples by the side of the sea of Galilee.

What do we need to know to make sense of this material?

Traditional historical criticism with its emphasis on what happened, how the tradition developed, and what were the circumstances of the final edition, would probably say that to understand the material fully we need to know something about the church for which the book was produced, and also something about the purpose of this Gospel. In this it has an ally with more recent sociologically inspired methods of criticism that seek details of the social world that produced the Gospel. An influential writer from this background has described the community of John as an example of sectarian Christianity. The Gospel seems to speak of a community that is exclusive, distinct from the world and which shares other ideological characteristics of a sect. The chief ethical injunction, for example, is to love one another. There's nothing here about loving enemies, and very little reference to outsiders at all. Most scholars would agree that John's church was a closed, male-dominated and esoteric community, perhaps without using the word 'sect', though it is difficult to ignore once you've heard it.

The purpose in writing may have been prompted by the expulsions from the synagogues already noted. This would explain the antagonism towards the Jews. It would also explain one of the main themes of the Gospel, which could be expressed as recognizing the truth when you see it. The opening chapter tells us that Jesus (the true light) was in the world, but neither the world nor his own people recognized him as such – and worse, they actually preferred darkness to light. This dualism between light and darkness, truth and falsehood, persists throughout the book, as does the theme of recognition. The writer uses the device of describing something obvious to the reader, but that the characters in question do not grasp. In chapter 3 Nicodemus is told he will have to be born again. (Actually this phrase is cleverly ambiguous. It can also mean, you must be born from above, as opposed to below – another example of John's dualism.) He misses any subtle point completely and asks how it can be possible to climb back into his mother's womb. This leader of the Jews thinks he has recognized Jesus, but he has not.

The purpose of the work is actually set out in chapter 20. The Gospel is written so that 'you may believe, that Jesus is the Christ, the Son of God, and that through this faith you may have life by his name'. Belief is equivalent to recognizing fully just who Jesus is. Doubting Thomas, who only appears in this Gospel, thinks that seeing is believing, but actually discovers that believing is seeing. It is faith that gives the insight to recognize truth. It is because of this overriding purpose that the Gospel is at such pains to point out who Jesus is. That could be said to be the central message of the book.

Who is Jesus?

For John, the most important thing is that Jesus is God. This is made clear in the opening poem, but in other places throughout the Gospel, we see the divinity of Jesus emphasized. At 5.18 we read how one of the reasons the Jews wanted him dead was that he was claiming equality with God – an interpretation of his previous words. At 10.30 he says quite clearly 'The Father and I are one.' This unity is an underlying theme of chapter 17 (see, for example, verse 5), and at 8.58 we have once again the defiant 'I am', in answer to a challenge: 'Before Abraham was, I am.' The strength of this claim has provided something of a problem for subsequent generations for whom the question, to what extent is Jesus both human and divine, has been important. To stress Jesus' divinity at the expense of his humanity is to suggest that he was really a kind of Father Christmas figure: divine, but prepared to dress up in human clothes. This is not good enough for Christians who want to understand Jesus' suffering as real, and who want him to be a genuine role model. Later generations of John's own church seem to have been somewhat confounded by this same problem, if we accept the evidence of the letters of John at face value.

As well as being God, John wants to portray Jesus as Messiah. That is, he stands firmly in the tradition of Jewish religion and can be understood in those terms. The claims that the Gospel makes are different from those of the Synoptic Gospels. Right from the start the disciples know who Jesus is. In the first chapter, Andrew says to Simon Peter his brother, 'We have found the Messiah.'

The place of Jesus in relation to the end of the age is interesting. There is no poetic description (such as that in Matthew 24 and 25) of how the age will end and how the Son of Man will then act. The assumption is that in this Gospel, as far as believers are concerned, all the decisive events in history important for salvation have already happened. In so far as there is a 'second coming', the Holy Spirit fulfils that function. Jesus' role is as the bringer of eternal life, and once the believer enters into that life, which is possible here and now, there is effectively no further stage in the process of salvation.

How can we use this material?

In order to make any use of it, we must recognize quite explicitly that large portions of the Gospel are reflections on the themes of Jesus' ministry that date from after the first Easter, and that these reflections come from a specific kind of religious community, which is hardly replicated in our world today. That being said, some of the reflections are mature and enduring, and some of the images, for example, the foot washing, have the power to move and motivate. The portion of the Gospel we are most likely to hear, is probably the first 14 verses, in a service at Christmas. In the service of Nine Lessons and Carols, this reading is introduced with the words, 'St John unfolds the mystery of the incarnation.' To my mind he actually compounds it, but the passage does enable us to compare the four Gospels. For Mark the proclamation of Gospel is the key opening note.

Matthew describes a context with his genealogy in chapter 1. Luke has a longer narrative section to set his context, and a genealogy that goes back not just to Abraham, as does Matthew's, but to the first human, Adam.

John also describes a new creation, but claims that Jesus was implicit in the first creation in the form of 'Word'. His appearance on earth represents Word made flesh. All Christians need to consider the problem with which the Gospel writers grappled, namely, how are we to understand Jesus in relation to our culture and history. How do we describe who he is?

In the Gospel, some of the most accessible pictures of Jesus are:

- *2.1–11 – here we see Jesus involved in ordinary community life.*
- *4.8–30 – one of the least stilted and yet playful conversations, which contains lots of theological pointers about the power and provenance of Jesus, and the way in which he supersedes previous religious understandings.*
- *6.1–15 – a very powerful re-telling of the loaves and fishes miracle. Unlike the kind of picnic conditions described elsewhere, this is full of tension and politically charged.*
- *10.14–16 – the picture of the good shepherd.*
- *11.1–43 – the raising of Lazarus containing some human vignettes of Jesus in a story that appears to combine earthy realism with incredible supernatural deeds.*
- *13.2–17 – the foot washing.*
- *14.1–6 – a relatively straightforward statement of what it means to be the divine Jesus.*
- *15.1–17 – emphasizes the interrelationship of Jesus with believers and their relationship with each other, using the image of the vine.*
- *Chapter 21 – a hopeful chapter in that it shows how Peter who had denied Jesus could be rehabilitated – a source of comfort for Christians throughout the ages.*

JOHN

You might like to read 📖 all these passages and rank them in order of accessibility.

- *Which might you commend to a friend who knows little about Christianity?*
- *Which appeals to you most?*
- *Which would you include if you were a film maker trying to assemble an hour-long documentary picture of Jesus' significance?*
- *Which would be most suitable as an introduction for children?*

The Gospel of John has long had a revered place in the Church. Likely as it is that the Christian beginner will find more to attract and inspire in the other Gospels, there are nonetheless enduring pictures of Jesus here, and a courageous attempt to reflect theologically on events that still puzzle and challenge.

12

Getting Started on the
Acts of the Apostles

The book of Acts (as it is commonly known) is a jolly good read, and perhaps as good a place as any, as has been suggested, to start to read the New Testament. It is the nearest the New Testament comes to something that looks like history, but it has many similarities with modern adventure stories. At face value it is a history of the Christian church from its beginnings on the day of Pentecost to the point where it has become truly international, though this account may not be quite as innocent as it looks. To write a history of the Church was almost as startlingly innovative as writing a Gospel. It makes a point about the author's faith in relation to the Church, since surely many people never thought that the Church would actually have a history. There is a scholarly consensus that the book is the second part of Luke's Gospel, and has the same author.

What's included?

Acts begins where Luke ended, with disciples in Jerusalem awaiting some significant new gift that will empower them. This gift arrives on the day of Pentecost. Luke names it as the Holy Spirit and describes it as the energizing force and presence of God that is responsible for the miraculous story that is about to unfold. That story (as Acts recounts it) begins in Jerusalem with accounts of the early Church's life and witness there. The key figure in the early part of the book is Peter, and we have detailed accounts of his preaching. As the Church grew there was need to provide a ministerial structure for growth, and chapter 6 begins to address this. Immediately afterwards we have an account of the first Christian martyrdom – that of Stephen.

This story provides us with a link to the rest of the book, in that one of the witnesses to Stephen's death was the man who had been zealous as a Jewish religious enforcer but who was soon to become Christianity's most famous convert – Paul. We have the first account of that conversion in chapter 9. (Others appear in chapters 22 and 26.) Thereafter we return to the story of Peter's leadership of the Church. Paul sets to work as a Christian missionary to non-Jews, and this proves hugely problematic and leads to a major debate about the future of the movement. The question at issue was whether potential converts from among the non-Jews had first to become Jews before they could become Christians (of which the main practical evidence for men would be circumcision); and that having become Christians whether they should be expected to adhere to Jewish practice. In other words, was Christianity simply one type of Jewish faith, a movement within Judaism?

The outcome of the discussion was that although Christianity was clearly descended from Judaism, nevertheless, it was something new and individual in its own right. The Christian claim was based on having found out new things about God's universality, and in practical terms this meant that it was international and with no special preference or privilege for former Jews. This decision had other theological implications, some of which we shall encounter in the letters of Paul. It is Paul who now takes centre stage. A series of missionary journeys, often in very exciting circumstances with a variety of narrow shaves and imprisonments, leads to expansion and success for the Church. New churches are founded, and Christianity develops from Palestinian obscurity to become a Mediterranean phenomenon.

However, just like Jesus before him, Paul is accused on trumped-up religiously motivated charges, and has to work his way through a tortuous legal system to try to prove his innocence. As a Roman citizen he is entitled to a hearing in Rome before Caesar himself, and this is what he opts for. We then have further exciting details of Paul's journey to Rome, complete with shipwrecks, and the book ends with Paul under a kind of house arrest in Rome, where he has full freedom to teach all comers to his lodgings all there is to know about God.

What do we need to know to make sense of this material?

Perhaps the first thing to consider is the genre of the work. What exactly is it? If indeed it is part 2 of Luke's Gospel, then the introduction in Luke 1.1–4, setting out the basis on which the piece was written, in effect stands as an introduction to the whole work, and gives us some clues. But just as we found that the Gospel (i.e. part 1) was not a simple disinterested recital of facts, but rather a theological work with a particular point of view that the author wanted to commend, then we might expect that the same thing will be true of Acts as part 2. Just as the Gospel gives a way of understanding Jesus and his significance, we might expect that Acts will do the same thing for the continuing Christian community. So what might he want us to believe?

The key dynamic of Acts is the inevitable and miraculous growth of the Church against all the odds. The book is set out almost as a staged account of growth with progress reports such as those at 6.7, 9.31, 12.24, 16.5, 19.20 and 28.31. The unwritten evangelistic appeal is: surely this is evidence that the Church is truly of God and not just human invention. What makes this claim so fascinating is that other evidence of this rapid and wholesale growth is difficult to find. What we actually see is a rather faltering Church, at the point where the first disciples are dying off – a likely time for the work to be written. Some scholars go as far as to accuse Luke of spin. His triumph they think is to persuade people who might think that the Church is failing in all sorts of ways, that it is in fact an incredible success story.

The first few chapters describe a church life that to anyone who has had experience of a faith community, appear idealistic to say the least, and probably quite unrealistic. In fact, the book itself reaches the same conclusion in effect. The experiment of having all things in common, acting only for the common good and really being diligent about a discipline of worship is difficult enough to maintain in a monastery, never mind a world in which Christians are a small minority and where they have to make a living, support families, further careers and so on. Although it doesn't actually describe it as a failed experiment in so many words, we hear very little about this form of church life in the rest of the book. Even the failures can somehow be counted as successes.

The next thing that is obvious is that Luke regards the arrival of Jesus and the development of the Church as significant events, not just in the life of the communities affected, but also in the history of the world. Some writers use the term 'salvation history' to describe the beliefs of those who understand human history in terms of the different ways that God has acted at particular points in time. One widely accepted example sees three periods in human history: the time of Israel, the time of Jesus and the time of the Church. It is an incredible claim to make, that the birth of an artisan in an obscure corner of the Roman Empire signals a key moment in world history, but that is what Luke does. All the world was present, he says, for the census that accompanied Jesus' birth. It is an even more amazing claim that the forming of the Christian Church should have a similar significance but once again on the day of Pentecost we read that Jews were there 'from every nation under heaven', and that what they witnessed was a reversal of Babel in Genesis 11. In that account, God confused people's languages, and the consequent misunderstanding and inability to communicate was considered a symptom of sin. In Acts 2, everyone understands what the apostles are saying. That symptom of sin has been overcome. Clearly, the term 'salvation' is one that has significance for Luke. Whereas neither Matthew nor Mark use it at all in their Gospels, it occurs eight times in Luke and nine times in Acts.

Another way of understanding history, deriving from the apocalyptic stable of writing, was to divide history into several ages in the belief that each age, and indeed the whole process, was designed by God, for a purpose. Most interest was focused on what happened at the end of one age and the beginning of another. (After all, there was little interest in living in the middle of an age when nothing was about to happen.) Different traditions describe how the transition from this age to the next will take place, in slightly different ways. Daniel 7.13 is a key text, apparently used a lot in religious circles around the time of Jesus, to describe the way in which those who are righteous in this age will be presented to God and vindicated. Someone called 'a son of man' transports the faithful on the clouds of heaven. There are elements of this text in several places in the New Testament, including Stephen's farewell speech (Acts 7.56). It probably contributed too, to the development of the parousia idea. This word 'parousia' is often translated 'second coming' but in fact its root meaning is far more elusive. However, it may have been the case that there were Christians who were expecting some new parousia/Daniel 7.13-type of intervention from God, after the first Easter, and it may be that this was an issue to which Acts was designed to make a contribution.

If you believe that history as we know it was about to come to an end with a new intervention from God, there is little point in developing the institutional life of a Church. In the past some scholars have thought that Matthew's Gospel was designed for this kind of audience. It was said to have no evidence of developed ministry, and the moral message it contained could only be suitable for a very short 'interim' period. Acts takes a very different view. Here we see a Church that is dug in for the long haul. New ministries, such as that of deacon are instituted and, in what we learn of Paul, we see someone developing a measured theology that will stand scrutiny in times other than those of fervent religious expectation. Moreover, it may be that Luke's account of the Ascension (which only occurs here) is meant to be an alternative interpretation of the parousia tradition.

We can see in Acts some of the features that characterized the Gospel of Luke. The universal interest of God and the universal availability of salvation, for example, feature in both works. We see also a strong pastoral flavour in Acts, reminiscent of the Gospel. Luke retains his interest in the business of the morality of wealth and property. Those who withhold wealth are punished (5.1ff.). On the other hand, through the deacons, there is a distribution to the poor signalling a responsible use of wealth (6.1–6). These kinds of example strengthen the links between Jesus and the Church, and this is itself an issue.

Some people have asked whether Jesus ever intended to found the kind of Church Luke begins to describe, or indeed that which we now have. Fairly quickly, an institution developed that Jesus might have had difficulty in recognizing, and Luke accepts that that needs to be argued for or defended. By describing the development of the Church as the work of the Holy Spirit, he maintains continuity and credibility. Some writers have pointed to other ways in which the author puts his argument that the Church is a legitimate development from the Jesus movement. The name of Jesus, for example, is an important element in salvation (e.g. 2.21, 4.12). It is a key element in situations of healing and forgiveness (3.6, 6.18, 9.34). The Word is also a means of continuity between Jesus and the Church (12.24, 13.26). It is also true that Jesus is made known in the actions of his followers.

Although it may be true that Acts is a work of theological persuasion rather than factual reporting, that is not to say that it does not contain evidence of things that happened, or that it is a totally unreliable source for learning more about early church life. The book does give us some insights similar to those we might gain from the Epistles, about subjects such as baptism, worship, fellowship, teaching, mission and church organization.

How can we use this material?

Probably the best place to start is the account of the founding of the Church in chapter 2. Read 📖 *2.1–21 and see how many of the themes we have identified you can see there. You might look for evidence that this Pentecost experience:*

- *Describes something that belongs, and can be understood in relation to, the tradition of the Old Testament;*
- *Is something significant for a wider group of people;*
- *Is momentous;*
- *Is capable of a number of interpretations, some of which are misunderstandings, and*
- *Has something to do with salvation.*

How satisfying do you find this account? Does it tie up loose ends of things that belonged to the realm of unfulfilled promise, in a way that enables you to go forward in anticipation of an unfolding story about a whole new way to understand the religious life in community (possibly what was intended for the first readers)? What would you expect to find next? What do you actually find?

Read 📖 *2.40–47, which describes the earliest expression of church. How attractive is the picture you find there? Have you any experience of attempts to live such a communal life, and if so how do they affect your response? How realistic is the expectation described? You might like to arrange to visit a religious community of monks or nuns and talk about how they see their role both within their own community and in the wider world. How might this picture translate into a modern setting? Does this make it any more realizable? Would it attract you? You might think about:*

- *Communal living*
- *A discipline that takes giving to the poor very seriously in a committed way*
- *A rule of life that includes prayer and service*
- *Membership of something like the Iona community, or the third order of Franciscans.*

How fair would it be to judge your local church by these standards?

The first account of martyrdom is interesting and worth reading. The whole incident stretches from 6.8 to 7.60 but you can get the gist of the action by reading 📖 *6.8–15 and 7.51–60. Most of the longer account is taken up with a long sermon setting out an interpretation of the Old Testament that is consistent with Christian understanding. This enrages Stephen's audience (much as Jesus' preaching did in the synagogue at Nazareth), and so they take him out and stone him.*

Accounts of martyrdoms were very popular at a later stage in Christian history, and often the details of what happened are presented in a way that will both interest and inspire the audience. They can also be a subtle way of making theological points. Note here, for example, the way the author links with the trial and death of Jesus, most particularly in Stephen's dying plea, 'Lord do not hold this sin against them' – reminiscent of Jesus' cry on the cross, 'Forgive them Father, for they do not know what they are doing.' The fact is that this was the first of very many cruel and savage deaths. But martyrs have a strange influence on movements. It was said later that, 'the blood of the martyrs was the seed of the church'.

What is your response to this account? Do you feel inspired or perhaps just saddened? Think of a modern martyr for the Christian or some other cause. Can you imagine telling their story in the idiom that Luke uses? What do you think is the 'value' of martyrdom?

Having seen God's power at work on the first Pentecost, in enabling the disciples to preach and empowering them to heal, in giving the Church confidence to grow and in inspiring martyrs, we now see the power of God to convert perhaps the most unlikely candidate imaginable. **Read** 📖 *Acts 9.1–9.*

What does the expression 'cradle Christians' mean to you? This is a phrase sometimes used to describe those who have been born into a Christian family and who have accepted that inheritance for themselves. This group is distinguishable from those who become Christians at a later stage in their lives. That group, in turn, divide between those who come gradually to faith and those whose acceptance of Christianity is a sudden and dramatic thing. What do you think are the relative merits of each of these ways of becoming a member? You might like to think about the importance of:

- *Being grounded in a family tradition*
- *Making decisions for yourself*
- *Having a well-thought-out faith*
- *Being able to point to a definite change of direction: a moment like marriage or the birth of a child when everything changed.*

In the nineteenth and early twentieth centuries, scholars of Acts were very consumed with the dispute about Jews and Gentiles. **Read** 📖 *11.1–18 to get a sense of the problem, and to see a way in which it was resolved for some. Sometimes a dispute in the Church can appear to be about something quite small and superficial, but actually be about a much bigger matter of principle. For example in the seventh century CE there was a big dispute in Britain, which on the surface was all about how you cut your hair, but was actually about two completely different ways of being church: the Roman and the Celtic. (The Roman way won.) On the face of it, this is all about male circumcision, but what do you think are the big issues involved here, and are they worth fighting about? If you thought of this as being about two different ways of being church what would each of the churches look like? Which one would you rather belong to?*

Finally, you might like to read another thrilling yarn about the adventures of **Paul** *in* 📖 *27.1—28.15. A century ago it was commonplace to see children's books recounting the thrilling adventures of missionaries, who were seen as quite glamorous people, akin to explorers. How do you think society views missionaries and Christian apologists today? Can you think of any way to re-introduce this kind of glamour to religion? In any case would it be desirable?*

In these last two passages we see the continuing major theme of the power of God – a power he has delegated to the apostles to an amazing degree. It is a power that reconciles, but chiefly it is the power that maintains the Church against all expectation.

13

Getting Started on the Letters of Paul

One of the most surprising things about Christian Holy
Scripture, and the New Testament part of it in particular, is the
form in which we find it. If we were devising a religion from
scratch, the likelihood is that we'd have a user-friendly guide to
Frequently Asked Questions, which would include clear statements of belief, an understandable account of ministry – who
does what and why, a whole series of instructions about how to
behave as well as how to order religious life, and some simple
ethical principles that could be applied without dispute to any
future problem in society. The New Testament is nothing like
this, even though occasionally some people treat it as if it were.
Most surprising of all is that a substantial part of it – well over
half if you count chapters – consists of a series of letters. What's
more, these letters have a very commonplace feel about them.
They speak of everyday things: people in common to the
authors and addressees and what's happened to them, places
visited, advice on problems encountered and so on. They are, in
truth, a poor resource for planning a systematic description of a
world religion, though that has not deterred some.

Apart from Acts of the Apostles (which could be considered a
sequel to a Gospel), and the book of Revelation (which does
actually contain seven letters within its text), the whole of the
New Testament apart from the Gospels consists of these letters
of varying length. Some of the most eloquent of these were
written by Paul. He was not one of the disciples and never met
Jesus in the flesh. As a result of his conversion though he became
the new religion's best-known advocate; so much so that some

people would regard him as the inventor of Christianity – the person who developed the communities that had gathered around the disparate fragments of oral tradition about Jesus' life and death into something with the potential to become an institution. Some people think that Jesus never intended to found a Church such as developed, and that what we have today is largely Paul's responsibility. Clearly then, it's important to know what he said, and how he said it.

What's included?

You might think that that is pretty obvious. After all, each of the letters describes, in its title, from whom it's come. However, this can be misleading. It might be more accurate to describe the contents of some letters ascribed to Paul, as *in the tradition* of Paul, since they were probably written after his death. It may be that some later authors wanted to claim the authority of Paul for what they wrote. The same is true, perhaps, of the letters ascribed to other famous figures. There is lively dispute, for example, about whether Peter wrote either of the letters that bear his name. In the case of Paul, there are some letters that we could describe as undisputed. There are some about which opinion is divided, and there is one, Hebrews, which is generally accepted as being written by someone other than Paul. The kinds of test that are applied to the letters to reach these conclusions are these:

- Is their vocabulary consistent with that of authentic letters of Paul?
- Are their theological ideas compatible with those of undisputed letters?
- Are they most similar to authentic letters of Paul or are they more like letters that were written some time after Paul's death, in their content or vocabulary?

This is more of an art than a science though, and conclusions are often reached with the help of a deal of subjective judgement. It is a problem to some Christians, in varying degrees, that Christian holy writ contains what appears to be some kind of disingenuity.

- The undisputed letters include: 1 Thessalonians, 1 and 2 Corinthians, Galatians, Romans, Philippians and Philemon.
- Slightly more controversial are 2 Thessalonians and Colossians.
- Much more controversial are Ephesians and the group of letters sometimes called the Pastoral Epistles, consisting of 1 and 2 Timothy and Titus.

For our purposes we shall consider the first two categories in this chapter, and the third category in the next.

As we look at the individual letters we need to bear some things in mind.

- All Paul's letters were written before the Gospels reached their final public form. The earliest probably dates from the late 40s of the first century CE, almost 20 years before the first Gospel.
- Paul was not writing for posterity. He was writing the kind of letters that respond to immediate circumstances.
- The content of the letters is not driven by some desire on Paul's part to make sure he's covered all the possible angles for some future enquirers about Christianity. It is, rather, a response to the particular issues that have arisen in the areas addressed, which cover a vast area of the then known world, and cross several cultural boundaries.
- Some of these letters have the flavour of replies. We can only guess at the originals.
- A collection of Paul's letters was in circulation by the second century (there is mention in 2 Peter 3.15 and 16 – probably the latest book in the New Testament).
- Paul is not referring to some other work of doctrine as he writes his letters. In other words, he is not using the letters to

deliver ideas of the truth about God: he is actually *developing* his ideas of the truth about God by participating in the corre- spondence with churches. The letters are a means of doing theology in their own right.

The main issue in the letters to the **Thessalonians** is one we see in the Gospels: How does Jesus relate to common religious expectation about an agent of God who will usher in a new age? The technical term most usually used to describe this area of interest is the Greek word parousia, which means, at its sim- plest, 'coming'. When this word is used in religious discourse it means more than that. It refers to the way in which God will vindicate or reward those who have stood by him in hard times, and so religious people suffering any kind of hardship, in Jesus' time, were particularly interested in it. Many of the signs of God's expected intervention in the affairs of the world were to be seen in Jesus' ministry, as the Gospel writers were quick to point out. They even use another technical term, 'resurrection', which until now had been mostly associated with the power of God to bring about the dawn of the new age, to refer to Jesus at the first Easter. But when would the parousia be? Had it hap- pened already, or was it still to come? Would Jesus come again specially to bring it about, or had he somehow already set in motion what it was meant to achieve? These were the kind of questions puzzling the Thessalonians. They even wondered whether it was worth continuing with normal working life if the end of the age was about to happen. There were other con- nected questions that also crop up elsewhere. What about people who have already died? Will they also have a reward as a result of what Jesus did? This kind of question is not now- adays at the top of most people's agendas, and so the issues in these letters can be a little difficult to connect with.

That is not the case with the letters to the **Corinthians**. It may be that there are as many as four letters contained in this material. It's here that we may think Paul would have been better off with e-mail, since he writes about a series of specific issues which need a quick response. He's also quite good at cut-and-paste as he imports, for example, a Christian hymn about love into a letter (1 Corinthians 13) to illustrate his point. Among the issues that take his attention are:

- What to do if a cult of personality develops in a church.
- What sexual behaviour is appropriate for Christians.
- Whether Christians are to have rules about food, as some religions do.
- How to conduct worship, particularly a eucharist.
- What is meant by spiritual gifts.
- What is Paul's take on the key term resurrection.
- Issues of pastoral care and ministry.
- Good practice in churches sharing resources.
- The issue of who has authority in the church, and with what credentials.

The Corinthian correspondence has been sub-titled by one writer, 'Being the Church in the World'.

Galatians comes across as a bit of a rant against a church that appears to have abandoned the faith Paul taught them, in favour of something he considers to be quite wrong. The issue here is about the radical newness of Christianity. For Paul, Christianity is a radical break from the basis of law on which Judaism operates. His argument is with those who want to see Christianity as a better form of Judaism with better laws and rules, rather than a complete alternative to this approach to religion. In the process we have some wonderful 'tight' writing that sets out how Paul sees the newness of Christianity. We see him using some of the key concepts of the new religion, such as the Holy Spirit, and the Grace of God, in a way that gives them clear shape and dynamic relevance.

It is generally agreed that Paul wrote **Philippians** from prison. Like other letters from prison (such as those from Dietrich Bonhoeffer, for instance) they have a particular character and force. This is mature writing about the nature of Christian life and discipleship.

The letter to **Philemon** is the only one written to an individual. It is a short note pleading the cause of a runaway slave, which gives some insight into Paul's pastoral concern, his authority within the community, and his understanding of Christianity as a religion of second chances.

Colossians (which may not be from Paul) deals with two areas of concern. The first is believing things that are not Christian as Paul understands it, and the second is right conduct. The letter includes a code of conduct for family members and slaves. The inclusion of this code is one of the reasons some people believe that Paul was not the author, since he does not usually write in this way.

Romans is generally regarded as Paul's most mature work and the one that comes nearest to being a theological treatise. Scholars throughout the centuries have regarded writing a commentary on Romans as their *opus magnum*. This deals with the place of the Christian Church within the history of religion, and particularly its relation to Judaism and the Old Testament. What are the implications for faith of Christianity's being a world religion? This is an appropriate theme for Christians in Rome, far away from Jerusalem and Palestine. It is also appropriate to write, as Paul does, about right relations with the state, and in service to wider society.

What do we need to know to make sense of this material?

The ways in which readers have tried to extricate meaning from the letters of Paul is a fascinating subject in its own right.

In the nineteenth century, some scholars, influenced by new Marxist ideas, thought that the key to understanding Paul was to see, in all his writing, evidence of the conflict in Galatians mentioned above. Paul was fighting a battle to preserve Christianity from those who would make it a traditional religion of rules and rites.

An aspect of this approach persisted into the twentieth century. That is, readers wanted to somehow connect what Paul wrote with the story of his own life, as it could be surmised from the letters, and especially Acts. The suggestion that Acts is a theological and not primarily a historical document, and the lack of consensus about conclusions that can be reached from reading the letters, has tended to make that approach less popular.

During the twentieth century it has been more common to try and systematize his writings under a number of headings. So, in a typical book there might be one chapter on grace, another on sin, a third on the Holy Spirit, and so on. This approach paid little attention to the specific location to which the letters were addressed.

The exact opposite was true for those who have believed, in the latter part of the century, that the key to understanding was to know more about the social structure of those places, and to apply methods of social scientific enquiry, using the letters as a key source.

More recently, scholars have moved away from scientific and historical methods of approach altogether, and looked at the letters as might students of literature. This has led to a new interest in, for example, exactly how Paul argues his case (what is his rhetorical strategy), on the one hand; and on the other, attempts to see in the letters a kind of 'Gospel according to Paul' (what is his narrative).

This variety of approaches can be rather daunting, so what are the main things we need to know to get started on Paul's letters? Here are three approaches for starters.

One thing we can look for is what the letters tell us about the development of the new religious community. It is in these letters that we see the discussions around the distinctive identity of followers of Christ. In what way will they imitate other religious systems to be found in the ancient world, and in what ways will they be completely different? This raises questions about organization, leadership, authority and hierarchy. Then there is the question of what this new constituency believes, again raising questions of authority – who is final arbiter of that? The fascinating thing here is to see how beliefs are developing, and how they are related, on the one hand, to reflection on the implications of Jesus' coming, death and resurrection as a whole; on the other, to see how they are related to the actual practical concerns of specific places and people. Questions of belief are of course connected to forms of worship, and those in turn are crucial for identity. Worship is a key way in which the new religion can be defined. In the letters we see Paul taking a lead on the conduct of eucharist / communion / mass, and we see a good deal of reflection about baptism. We get a real insight into the key ethical questions of the day as well. Are Christians going to be defined by the view they take on these, and will their community life be affected as a result? Scholars have become a little wary about treating the letters as reliable historical sources for some purposes, but that does not prevent them from being a fascinating window on to a religious ferment, teeming with life and controversy as a new religious constituency is born.

The second thing we might bear in mind is that these are *letters* – they are a specific means of communication that have both possibility and limitation. Letters are dynamic, personal and immediate. They deal with ordinary life. They have a provisional nature. They point to a desire to communicate, and to hold together different communities and points of view within some kind of coalition. The letters are a means of commending good practice, giving pastoral support, maintaining some kind of uniform approach to issues, developing dialogue and maintaining fellowship.

The third thing is that when people point to Paul as 'the inventor of Christianity', what they observe is that Paul considers the Christian story, not as someone who was caught up in the immediate events of Jesus' ministry, but rather as someone who took a wider perspective on what Jesus' coming and death might mean for our unfolding understanding of the story of God. What new things do we learn about God from the fact that he took an initiative to save the world from itself; and that in the process he was crucified? And what implications are there in all this for the religious community? This is a huge subject but some of the fundamental points for Paul are these.

- God abandoned power for weakness. It is no longer possible for there to be a religious view that sees God as an almighty fixer, and organizer of the universe. No one could believe in God in the old way and accept that he had been crucified – something that Paul often stresses. Moreover, this was God's initiative, and his sacrificial act of friendship or love towards the world was deliberate. It was his act of faith in humankind. The technical term for this behaviour is 'grace'.
- Grace is necessary because humankind does not have the resources, without God, to save itself. There can therefore be no religious view that sees human religious observance as having any effect on what God does. The old view that humankind could somehow make the world safe, and consolidate individual futures, by making the right sacrifices, performing the correct rituals and keeping the appropriate laws and rules has been superseded.
- A religion, such as Judaism, that focuses on adherence to the law as an instrument of salvation is therefore completely misguided.
- The principle of grace is one that should control all human social behaviour as well.
- The understanding of God as the one who takes graceful initiatives leads also to an understanding that all we have and do and achieve is by the grace of God and not as the result of our own intellect, power or desert. To this extent our characters and the achievements they lead to, are gifts from God. We have responsibilities to recognize these gifts and use them for the common good.

In his writings, Paul applies these understandings to questions he is asked, for example, about religious observance, worship, church organization and social ethics. He is very aware of how revolutionary this understanding is. It turns traditional religious expectation on its head. (That is: the expectation that I can secure my place in eternity by following the rules, and that a powerful God will then reward me.) He also attempts to 'translate' this vision into the received religious categories, vocabulary and thought forms, both of Judaism, and of other religions found throughout the Greek-speaking world. All of this means lots of re-interpretation of traditional terms like resurrection, parousia and salvation.

How can we use this material?

If you're coming at this from a traditional view of religion, there's a lot to get your head around here, and it's worth looking at some passages where Paul is trying to persuade an audience that hasn't quite got hold of the idea yet.

Read 📖 *1 Corinthians 1.18–2.5. Here Paul is talking to people who want to develop a church on lines that mirror the social class structure of ordinary society. Paul says that from the perspective of 'the world', the story of Jesus and his crucifixion simply demonstrates the weakness of God and the foolishness of God. Then look at* 📖 *Philippians 2.5–11. This is a famous passage, possibly quoting an early Christian hymn of which Paul approves. Again he stresses how God 'emptied himself' and how that action should lead to a reappraisal not only of God but of human relationships as well. Finally, read* 📖 *Colossians 2.6–15. Here Paul refers to teachings of other religious systems that he urges his hearers to reject. Baptism is the new Christian rite that acknowledges all God has done, including (in a memorable phrase) nailing the old way of being religious with its laws and demands to the cross (my paraphrase of verse 14).*

You might think about what this means in practice today. When a disaster of some kind occurs, the cry goes up: How could God allow this? What does Paul's view of God have to say as an answer do you think? Or again, what would a Church and what would a society look like, that really took Paul's view of human achievement as a gift from God seriously? Is it possible to have that degree of humility in public life? Can you think of any positive thing to be said for a God that is weak as opposed to one that is strong?

If you have contact with a church you might like to read some of the critical things Paul has to say about church organization, and to compare your own experience with that. A good place to start might be to **read** 📖 *1 Corinthians 11.17–22. 1 Corinthians is very accessible for this purpose. Chapter 12 has lots to say about how different gifts should be understood and used. Do you belong to any group that operates on this understanding?*

Read 📖 *Galatians 5.13–end. Here Paul is developing the view that the old view of religion is one that treats us like children rather than adults, and that it is restrictive and closed. He regards the Christian alternative as representing freedom and maturity. The danger in such a view is that the freedom could be abused, and here we see him setting out the practical implications as he sees them, so as to be clear what he does and does not mean. Today in Britain we hear a lot about the 'nanny state' and about the need for more laws. Does Paul's view have any contribution to make to that debate? A similar passage is to be found at* 📖 **Colossians** *3.12–17. This is sometimes read at weddings. Why do you think it might be suitable?*

This is just a brief flavour of the contribution of someone whose passion was to communicate the significance of a loving graceful God who could be crucified. As far as he was concerned, nothing in religion or the history of thought would ever be the same again.

14

Getting Started on the Other Letters

For the most part, the authors of the remaining letters of the New Testament are unknown. Quite a lot of scholarly energy has been spent in trying to identify some of them, so as to apply to them the same kind of questioning that could be applied to the known letters of Paul. However, the tendency now is to accept that such attempts depend inevitably on personal conjecture, that there is very little known that would be helpful about any of the supposed authors, and that it is better simply to let the documents speak for themselves. The most that can be said is that some of these letters belong to a particular tradition: of Peter or John, or Paul himself. Others defy such classification. Like the letters of Paul, these letters give us a chance to see how the nascent Christian community responded to changing circumstances; and give us some insight into the kinds of personality that shaped the movement for centuries to come. These letters appear to have been written later than those of Paul and show us a different stage of development, in which different issues have come to the fore. They demonstrate the huge variety and diversity of the earliest Christians. In Paul's letters we saw this in terms of the addressees. In these letters we see it also in terms of the authors. But no less in these letters than in Paul's we open a window on what it means to be a new faith community.

What's included?

Basically, everything that isn't a Gospel, or Acts, or the Book of Revelation or the letters we dealt with in the last chapter. Some of these documents, such as 3 John for example, are rarely read in public. Others that belong to the same category include 2 John, 2 Peter and Jude. Some of the letters belong to small sub-groups. There are three letters ascribed to John and two to Peter. The group that consists of 1 and 2 Timothy and Titus are known as the Pastoral Epistles. Hebrews and James stand alone. Ephesians is the closest to Paul, and may, indeed, have been written by him.

The themes of 1 **Peter** are suffering, worship and Christian behaviour. In proportion to its length, this book contains more references to suffering than any other letter. It also contains several references to baptism, along with a number of phrases suggestive of later liturgies. This has led to theses that 1 Peter is really a liturgy dressed up as a letter; or at the very least a sermon for a baptism, perhaps even one devised for use on Easter Sunday. Probably the most famous passage is 2.4–10 in which the letter describes the people of God as 'living stones . . . being built into a spiritual house to be a holy priesthood'. The most radical interpretation of this passage sees it describing something completely new in Christianity, in terms of its superseding the old religion of buildings, hierarchies and rituals. From now on the Christian community as a whole will assume this role. The idea of a 'priesthood of all believers', very popular among Reformers like Luther in the sixteenth century, finds its strongest expression here. There are several passages in the letter that describe desirable conduct. One, at the beginning of chapter 3, conforms to what is called a 'household code', of which there are other examples in the New Testament. Elsewhere some commentators have seen similarities between some of the teaching material in 1 Peter, and that in other letters, such as Ephesians, which may suggest a common store of such material, possibly generally used for catechumens –

those learning about Christianity prior to their baptism as adults.

Ephesians shows sufficient similarity with the letters of Paul for him to be seriously considered as its author. Whether or not this is the case, it certainly stands in his tradition. It lacks some of the personal touches of the other letters; it includes what looks like traditional early Christian material (see above on 1 Peter), and may have been intended for more than one congregation. It is certainly intended for a primarily non-Jewish, or Gentile audience. It has some similarities with Colossians in that both paint a picture of the Church and its current situation against a backcloth of global destiny and cosmic significance. Its most accessible theme is that of unity, more strongly stated here, probably, than anywhere else in the New Testament. This unity has a cosmic dimension – it is God's final intention for creation; it has a Jewish/Gentile dimension, and it has a dimension within Christian congregations. In one of the best-known passages, Ephesians 4.11–14, the author describes how individual gifts are to employed within the body of Christ for the common good. This possibility of unity is closely related to the work of Jesus, and is one result of his death on the cross. That being said, Ephesians is more concerned about the Church than the work of Jesus as such.

The so-called **Pastoral Epistles** of 1 and 2 Timothy and Titus are less likely to be from Paul, though in older versions of English Bibles, they are ascribed to him. The name derives from the fact that they appear to be addressed to individual pastors, and deal with everyday issues encountered by church leaders. Sociologists are interested in what these letters tell us about the developing life of Christian communities, and there has been some interest in the thesis that 2 Timothy in particular offers a kind of spiritual direction. As in Colossians we are made aware of the need to be on our guard against heretics, particularly against those who think that the truth has only been revealed to the few, rather than to all (see 1 Timothy 2.4, for example).

Once again there are codes. In fact 'order' is very much a theme of the group. The Church is described as 'the household of God', giving rise to a charge that these letters display a kind of bourgeois attitude towards Christianity modelled on secular households with strict hierarchical rules and attitudes.

The letter of **James** takes us into different territory. James' concern is that religion can be a very airy-fairy thing and quite self-indulgent. What makes the difference is whether or not faith leads to practical action. Faith without works, in his view, is worthless. This is a 'Catholic Epistle', so-called because it is addressed generally rather than to a specific church or audience, and it did have a bit of a struggle both to achieve the kind of general acceptance that enabled it to get into the New Testament in the first place, and to retain any status there. One recent publication wonders whether we should consider it as the junk mail of the New Testament. The main reason is its lack of reference to Jesus. He is referred to just as a teacher, and then only three times. Also, there is no mention of the bigger themes of salvation; no excitement about a new revelation of God, or of adventurous and innovative exploration of what new possibilities there are for the Church or for religious life as a result. However, there are those who think the letter is a concise statement of Christian ethics and who see many parallels between James, and Jesus' teaching in the Synoptic Gospels. The letter has some similarities with Old Testament wisdom writing, but is more subversive than that, favouring the weak, poor and landless. One of the most frequently heard passages is that about prayer for and with the sick, at 5.13–18.

On the face of it, the letter to the **Hebrews** is one of the most inaccessible documents of the New Testament. It is written in a style that is difficult, conveys ideas that are quite outside our present reality, and all in a letter about whose circumstances of writing hardly anything is known, including information about the author or recipients, or indeed whether it is even a letter at all. On the other hand, it is extremely theologically creative and actually appears to have been written by someone with a very strong pastoral sense. The pastoral situation is one in which a once active Christian community has effectively become disheartened and depressed, and so has abandoned the very things which give Christian communities their identity, such as assembly and worship. The author is interested in these people as people and does not have a well-worked-out doctrine of the Church as such, though he does have something to say about discipleship. What he tries to do is excite his audience with an innovative presentation of Christianity, which develops a number of themes around Jesus as an aid to encouragement.

The three **letters of John** are reminiscent of the style of the Gospel of John. They employ the same theological motifs such as light and life. 2 and 3 John, very short notes really rather than letters, are both concerned with the treatment of itinerant preachers and the issue of hospitality. It is 1 John that sets the scene for these two letters and contains most theological interest. What is really interesting, though, about this collection is the insight it gives us into inter-church conflict. In the Gospel of John, the enemy is 'the Jews' or 'the world', whereas in the letters, the enemy is another church who now embody all that is implied by 'the world'. The first area of dispute between the author of the letters and his opponents is about the person of Jesus.

One of the key areas of Christian debate in the early period was around the issue of: to what extent was Jesus both human and divine? If you erred on the side of considering him more man than God, then you ran the risk of downplaying his eternal significance. If you erred on the side of considering him to be mostly God but taking human form, you ran the risk of denying his actual human suffering – a key element of Christian distinctiveness. The Gospel of John comes close to this latter position to an extent that you can well imagine followers who depended on that Gospel as their text having a rather other-worldly view of religion. This is what 1 John wants to correct (see for example 1 John 4.1–3). Allied to this is a debate about ethics.

Christian faith must be grounded in practical acts of brotherly love. What is notable, however, is that this love appears to be confined exclusively to the group, the brethren, rather than the neighbour or the stranger.

2 **Peter** and **Jude** are related to each other. The generally accepted view is that 2 Peter draws on Jude as a source. Both are concerned with false teachers. 2 Peter is the book that had the biggest struggle to attain New Testament status. Some scholars think it to be as late as 135 CE. It has a particular style related to a genre, familiar at the time, sometimes known as 'the farewell speech' in which some worthy issues a summary of true belief in the face of his imminent death, with warnings about future distortions.

What do we need to know to make sense of this material?

Not long ago, the scholarly approach to this material was designed mainly to piece together an historical picture of how the early Church developed. It was therefore very important to know as much as possible about the historical circumstances of each of the letters, and great care was taken to try to discern the author, place and circumstances of writing, and destination of each of the letters. Three things could now be said about this approach.

At one level it simply failed to deliver. Take, for example, 1 Peter. As recently as 40 years ago two influential commentaries were published on this Epistle. One dated it in the seventies of the first century; the other dated it around the year 112. In the second half of the last century, commentators generally were not agreed about who wrote it, why it was written, whether it was a unity, whether the sufferings described in it referred to state persecution or civil harassment or whether they were illustrative of some kind of 'spiritual' suffering. Almost any date between 64 and 120 was suggested, with at least three different possibilities for authorship. Some thought it to be a letter. Others thought it a liturgy, a sermon, two sermons tagged together or a letter attached to a sermon. Given these sort of results, the quest for an historical base was clearly misguided.

Sometimes this historical quest was allied to the belief that the Church grew in a pretty unified kind of way. Some thought that it was possible to discern in the New Testament letters, a stage called 'early Catholicism' with a kernel of agreed doctrine and practice that would form the heart of what would become 'Christianity'. In more recent times the unity of the early Church has been severely questioned, not least on the grounds that the letters paint a completely different picture of the early years of the Church. Of the 27 books of the New Testament, it is sometimes claimed that at least 24 would never have been written if there hadn't been an argument going on. What the letters bear witness to is not so much unity, as diversity. Some of the letters show just how bitter this was. The letters of John are written by those whose view prevailed – that is, if you like, by the winners – and there is little sympathy for the losers. When one thinks of church controversies nowadays such as that over the ordination of women in the Anglican Church, and the care that was taken to make sure adequate pastoral provision was made for those who disagreed with the decision, the letters of John make almost embarrassing reading. Opponents are described as heretics and anti-Christs who are not to be welcomed or allowed to speak or teach. They were probably quite nice people really. Even where different congregations co-existed they sometimes had different vocabularies for expressing their faith, different priorities within the faith, different ways of organizing church life, and so on. It suited some church writers (Luke for example in Acts) to present a picture of a unified and purposeful church, but the reality was probably very different, and any approach that assumes too much is bound to reach suspect conclusions.

The third thing that one might ask is: Am I bothered? What difference does it make whether the letters of John were written by the author of the Gospel? So what if Peter didn't write 1 Peter or 2 Peter? Does it really matter whether Galatians was sent to

north Galatia or south Galatia? The emergence of pastoral and
practical theology has demanded that texts be read in a way that
is pastorally useful, and that means that questions that might be
important to a textual historian are not necessarily those that
are asked by people who want to make sense of the material
from the point of view of their own discipleship.

That is not to say that we can divorce ourselves completely
from history if we want to access the meaning of the texts. It is
still possible to see certain trends in this later material, which
suggest historical contexts that do have pastoral potential. One
anthropologist, for example, sees a definite movement through
the tradition of Paul's letters that describes different stages of
institutionalization. In the genuine letters there is community
building. In the slightly later disputed letters like Ephesians
there is community *stabilizing*, and in the later Pastorals there
is community *protecting*. Is the Church inevitably subject to
this kind of movement, and which stage represents the true
Church? Throughout history there have been attempts, from
the Protestant Reformation to the House Church Movement
of the 1960s, to get back to the initial creative community-
building adventurous stage of theology. Are these attempts
always doomed to result eventually in a new protected tomb?
These questions have a bearing on the weight placed upon
tradition and on the way we argue the case for change in the
Church today.

If we are to think of themes that give us clues about the main
concerns of the emerging Church, then the following would
probably feature on any list.

- The letters continue to give us examples of *new pictures of
  church and its ministry*. Nowadays it is commonplace to
  speak of 'new ways of being church' and 'mission-shaped
  church' and we expect a degree of provisionality and experiment about them. Somehow we do not expect the same thing
  in the New Testament, but that is indeed what we find. 1
  Peter is one of the most radical with its assertion that priesthood is now not the preserve of a human individual but is

somehow vested in the whole community of believers. The letters of John show us what a different model of church looks like, organized on more egalitarian lines with little hierarchy, and with a belief that all the important events in the history of salvation have already happened, as opposed to those who think that there is some other imminent 'coming' which Christians should expect.

- They show that the main *areas of controversy* are around the question of how to describe Jesus' significance. What does it mean to say that he is Christ or Lord or Son of God, or that he is both human and divine? Allied to this are questions about whether there is to be some future 'coming' and what the implications are in all this for a distinctively Christian mode of behaviour.

- Questions about *authority* begin to emerge after the first generation of disciples begin to die off. When there is a dispute, how is it to be resolved? Whose word is law? Is it possible to have a Christian Church without some kind of authority structure? This raises questions also about Scripture as a means of authority, and what books should be contained in a new canon of holy works. We see the beginnings of creeds, liturgies and teaching material that may have been used and accepted as normative in a number of different churches.

- Questions about *unity and diversity* are not restricted to debates within Christianity. They have a bearing on the continuing questions about the relation between Christianity and Judaism. To what extent is the former a development of the latter, and to what extent is there a completely new start?

- There are issues around *maintaining momentum*. It was easy for the first disciples and Paul to feel excited, but how is that to be experienced a couple of generations later? Is it by encouraging the expectation of an imminent return, for example? Or is it by keeping controversy boiling? Perhaps it is by putting lots of energy into developing a new order and constitution. Or, as in the case of Hebrews, is flagging interest to be countered by creative and slightly off the wall theology?

For the most part, these letters do not offer us stunning new insights into theology. Unlike the genuine letters of Paul they do not attempt to find creative and imaginative new ways of speaking about the discoveries that are made when we reflect on how a strong God became weak and human and was eventually crucified. What these letters do attempt to explore is what it means to be able to attach the description 'Christian' to any enterprise, and that is a very contemporary issue. There is no copyright on the term 'Christian', and many people use it in a way that scandalizes other Christians. These letters show us the roots of the issues that surround that problem.

How can we use this material?

Here are some suggestions.

To get a sense of the social setting of some early Christians, and how that has determined the text to an extent, read 📖 *1 Peter 2.11–25. The folk to whom this is addressed were people without residence rights, down at the bottom of the social scale. Nowadays, we might compare them with asylum seekers or immigrants with limited work permits. What evidence can you find for that in the passage? Imagine yourself as one of them, as best you can. What is your reaction to what is written? What would be the most important thing about Jesus as far as you were concerned?*

Now read 📖 *1 John 2.1–11. Imagine yourself as part of a distinct, perhaps fairly separate, religious community. You are neither suffering nor persecuted. Life is just ordinary. Your community is concerned about religious truth. From reading this passage what would Jesus mean to you, and how would that differ from the 1 Peter Christian? Does it matter that these differences exist, and if so how could you overcome them?*

Read the 1 John passage again and then **read** 📖 ***James 4.13–17 and 5.1–6.*** *Is there a difference in the priorities of these two writers? What does each consider to be sinful? To whom is each asked to pay special attention? Which do you find the more compelling?*

Read 📖 **Hebrews 6.1–8** *and try to imagine the situation to which it is written. Does it remind you of any situation you know? How would you describe the writer's response to it?*

To get a sense of the direction of things **read** 📖 **1 Timothy 2.** *This describes order within the Church and between the Church and the state. Imagine how this might have been different if Paul himself had written it early in his ministry, or how James might have put it. What do you think is the right relation between Church and state? Has the religious community got it right today? What are the implications for, for example, church schools, or church leaders sitting in the House of Lords?*

To get a sense of the importance of 'Christology', that is, the specific significance of Jesus, think of three films in which Jesus has figured that you have seen. What would a neutral member of the audience have taken away with them about Jesus from each film? How wide a range of pictures of Jesus' significance do you think it is possible or desirable to have within Christianity? Does thinking like this help you to appreciate the problem faced by early Christians?

Finally, can you think of one belief that you have seen in religious circles, that you would be willing to consider a complete heresy, and that might prompt you to write as strongly as did the author of 1 John? What makes it a heresy, and how would you defend your view? What are the plusses and minuses of such robust exchange? Does your thinking help you relate to the arguments in these letters?

15

Getting Started on Revelation

The last book of the Bible is one of the least accessible to a reader who is just getting started. At first sight it looks like a mixture of Dan Brown and Harry Potter, with descriptions of strange creatures, coded messages, conflict between the powers of good and those of evil, and fantastic visions in which it seems the faithful have a starring role. And yet, perversely, this is a book that even beginners are often anxious to get started on. The word 'Revelation' is a translation of the Greek title of the book, *Apocalypsis*, or as it is sometimes transliterated, 'Apocalypse', and that word and its derivative 'apocalyptic' do have a hold on the popular imagination. Unfortunately, that is largely through misuse, and those who come to the book expecting to find coded information about the date and circumstances of the end of the world are going to be disappointed. That being said, this is a book with lots of contemporary reference and interest.

What's included?

The book is 22 chapters long. After a brief introduction, chapters 2 and 3 contain a series of seven letters addressed to churches in what would nowadays be western Turkey. Although we don't usually refer to Turkey when we speak of 'the holy lands', we might well. Great Christian centres like Ephesus are to found there, and it's likely that it was a stronghold of early Christianity. The seven churches are all in cities, and the writer appears to have detailed knowledge both of the cities and their heritage, and of the life of the churches within them. He makes cryptic references to aspects of each city's life. This gives the letters the appearance of clever poetic review or appraisal summaries of each of the churches. For example, Laodicaea, the one church for which there is nothing but criticism, was an important banking and financial centre. It had a reputation for healing eye diseases, and it was renowned for its production of ready-made clothing – a kind of combination of Zurich, Moorfields Hospital and Leeds. The writer describes the church there as naked, blind and poor. There are only good things to say about the church in Philadelphia. The remaining five have both plus and minus points.

From here on there is a change of tone. Chapters 4 and 5 both contain visions that have a strong dramatic and liturgical flavour. Their theme is creation and victory. This is followed in chapters 6 through to 8 by visions of seven seals. The backcloth to this vision is worship in heaven. That continues to be the backdrop in chapters 8 to 11, which describe the vision and audition of the seven trumpets. The theme of seven continues through to the end of chapter 16, with an exposé of evil perceived through the drama of the seven last plagues and the seven bowls of the wrath of God. Chapter 18 is a lament, or perhaps a celebration of the fall of Babylon, the earthly symbol of evil. Chapters 19—22 contain seven visions of the end of the age, culminating in the new Jerusalem. Chapter 22 has further concluding remarks.

What do we need to know to make sense of this material?

What is an apocalypse?

The first thing we need to know is what it means to call a book 'apocalyptic'. For Bible readers this is a very precise term that refers to a series of written works that developed within Judaism and Old Testament religious culture from about the second century BCE and continued in both Judaism and Christianity until about 150 CE. In the Old Testament, the book of Daniel is the best example. In the New Testament, Revelation is the only complete apocalypse, though there are other briefer examples of the style in the Gospels (in Matthew chapter 24 for example). It is difficult to give a very precise definition of apocalyptic, though if you read several of them you get the flavour of the genre and learn how to recognize it. These are very carefully crafted written works. They are not reports of things said, or narratives containing a story line, though they do have a dramatic movement. The best way to recognize an apocalypse is probably through its literary characteristics.

Apocalypses:

- Make a big deal of secrecy. The word means 'revelation', and that which is revealed is nothing less than secrets within history, really known only to God. They are written as if these secrets have been revealed to some special person from history, to give them greater effect.
- Are full of symbols. Some of these are fantastic creatures. Some of them, such as 'lamb' or 'vine' have Old Testament connotations. Some colours are symbolic in the same way that they are today. White, for example, signifies purity and innocence. Numbers are also symbolic. We might think of these writers like primitive scientists, trying to unlock the secrets of creation and frantically searching for numbers that appear significant. Four is an obvious one. There are four corners of the earth and four winds. Seven is even more obvious because there are seven days in a week. In fact seven is deeply embedded in many cultures as significant. Many folk tales tell of giants in seven-league boots, or heroes who sail the seven seas. In apocalypses, seven is a number of God. Hebrew allows us to 'intensify' this, so that the most perfectly divine being we can imagine would have the number 777. In contrast if we were to think of an impostor, someone who claimed to be God but isn't, then his number might be six; one short of seven. If we were to think of the ultimate such

impostor, we could give him the number 666. Get the idea?

- Usually claim to be written by some famous person from the past, though Revelation is an exception to this.

- Are concerned with describing history as if it had all been designed in advance by God, and split into different bite-size 'ages'. Most interest centres on how we shall know when one age is about to come to an end and another one begin.

- Have a very strong moral content. Indeed some such writings take the reader on a kind of trip through hell just to demonstrate how awful is the fate of those who make the wrong choices in life. There are lurid, almost obscene, descriptions of the punishments meted out to the wicked. By contrast, of course, there is lavish reward for those who do right.

- Present God as a bit of a distant figure. He is viewed often as a kind of distant prime minister who has delegated some functions to other cabinet ministers. Raphael is minister for health, Michael minister for war, Gabriel minister for communication and so on. The effect is to find angels (the root meaning of the word is, 'messengers') cropping up all over the place. God does not communicate clearly to the faithful through current events, but often through dreams, some of which interpret events.

Apocalypses in their setting

A consequence of all this is that apocalypses describe reality as if there were two different but related spheres: that of earth and that of heaven. What happens in each affects the other. This is one of the main mechanisms of Revelation. John sees and hears things from the heavenly realm, but they mirror what's happening on earth.

It's important to know that apocalyptic writing is a response to a particular kind of question asking. In the Old Testament, we read how the Israelites went into exile, and how that experience of trauma and suffering prompted them to discover new things about God. Chief among their discoveries was that there is just one God, and it seemed to follow from that, that if there were just one God, and if he were creator of heaven and earth, then he was surely also the creator and designer of history. This might seem like a very comforting and majestic thought, but it does raise questions. If God designed our world and our history, why is there so much suffering? And especially why do good and faithful people suffer? Why do strong and warlike nations conquer the meek? Apocalyptic writing comes from situations where religious people cannot understand why God seems so distant, so mute and so unresponsive in the face of their suffering or persecution. It is particularly appropriate when it is possible to identify an enemy: a group or a nation which seems to stand opposed to all that God's people support, to the extent that they can be said to epitomize evil.

If we can put ourselves in the position of people like that we shall be able to understand this way of writing better. Some of the most illuminating writing about apocalyptic has come from such people. For myself, my experience of living in a mining community during the 1984 miners' strike helped me a lot. In this situation, for example:

- Issues were described in black and white terms. Decisions had to be made. Were you for us or against us?
- Propaganda regularly idolized our side and demonized the other side.
- There was a feeling that what was at stake was more than what was obvious. This was a key moment in history – a time of significance.
- Those who were considering returning to work as 'blacklegs' were a special concern. The consequences of their possible actions were painted in graphic terms.
- This was regarded as essentially a moral struggle and not just an industrial dispute.
- There was a tremendous feeling of vulnerability and powerlessness.

These all feature in the psychology of apocalyptic. Times are described as significant in God's plan. This is a moral fight in which the ultimate enemy is evil itself. And yet the whole thing seems overwhelming with the danger of giving up the fight (in religious terms, the danger of abandoning God for another, that is the danger of *idolatry*) or even of joining the other side because it seems so attractive in the short term (in religious terms, the danger of *immorality*).

The apocalyptic message

What apocalyptic says to people in this situation is that although faith seems at odds with experience and although God seems very distant, in fact God is on the case. These present difficulties are a necessary part of bringing a bigger plan to fruition. That bigger plan involves the history of the world and the dawn of a new age in the near future. The thing is to hang on in there and not to succumb to either immorality or idolatry because the consequences will be dire. In the new age everything will be different and there will be justice for those who are presently denied it. There will be vindication for those who have persevered and kept faith, and punishment for enemies. Evil will finally be conquered. Pain and suffering will finally be things of the past. And in the new dispensation, the kingdom of God, there will be no more tears, but there will be a new kind of citizenship for the faithful.

A number of these ideas are recognizable from elsewhere in the New Testament, and especially in the Synoptic Gospels, which are heavily influenced by apocalyptic thinking. In Revelation, as a Christian apocalypse, the emphasis is a little different. What this says is that Jesus has actually won the battle against evil already (on the cross), but its effects have yet to filter through. The important thing is to believe in the victory. The story of Jesus' triumph over evil is introduced in apocalyptic terms in chapter 5.

Christians in Asia

It follows from this that one of the key things to know in order to make sense of the material, is something about the actual situation of the writer and addressees. Apocalyptic flourished in this period in Judaism precisely because the nation was under occupation by alien powers, and the indigenous religion and culture was threatened by powerful tyrannical states. Very often these states were simply given the title 'Babylon', as a reminder of the awful experience of the Jewish people in exile there. In the same way, nowadays we use the term, 'holocaust' to describe all kinds of unimaginable evil perpetrated by humans against their fellows. In Revelation 'Babylon' equals Rome, but could also stand for any similar power in other circumstances and times.

The people to whom this book was addressed also felt vulnerable and powerless. For them too, God's declaration of victory seemed hollow, given their circumstances. They too were in danger of falling away to idolatry or immorality.

In social terms these Christians were suspect on a number of counts.

The Jews were suspicious of them because they were afraid that the Roman authorities might confuse Christians with themselves. The Jews had won certain concessions from the Roman state with regard to Sabbath observance, organizing synagogue life, and service in the army and they were anxious not to lose these rights if Rome became annoyed with the Christians. Of course there was an even more basic theological divide in that Christians and Jews both believed they knew the truth about the one God.

The ordinary population of these places in western Turkey (or Asia Minor as it was known then) considered the Christians a threat to good order. This was a time of peace and prosperity in the area, and those who enjoyed that, believed that they had Rome to thank. This thankfulness took several forms. Prominent people might erect statues to Roman heroes for example. More controversially, people might be required to go through some quasi-religious ritual involving the goddess Roma – the personalization of the state. They gladly accepted the hand of the state in their lives as an acceptable price to pay, but not so the Christians who sometimes refused to do what many people regarded simply as acts of loyal citizenship. The area was prone to both earthquakes and famines, and it was natural then to scapegoat Christians when things went wrong. ('We're suffering like this because those Christians didn't offer the right sacrifices to the Roman state gods.') All of this meant that the state itself looked on Christians with suspicion, and we have evidence of periodic witch hunts.

Christian insistence on there being only one God was completely at odds with a popular culture that saw no problem in having lots of them. Religious and cultural pluralism was a hallmark of the region under Roman rule. In some localities then there were problems that led to suspicion and harassment.

From a Christian perspective, the state was anything but benign. Its outward face masked corruption, injustice and a morality at odds with Christian beliefs. Its exercise of power was seen as an abuse to an extent that the state became coterminous with evil itself. Complacent people needed to be warned of this. This apocalyptic writing gave an idiom in which the clear distinctions between state and community of Christian faith could be drawn, and in which the dangers could be described. To Christians, a powerless minority, this was a clear vision, but there seemed no way of realizing the power of God as against the evident power of the state. Talk of Christ's victory must have seemed hollow to those who could see only evidence of the state's power, evidence in their terms of the victory of power, might and evil. Again, apocalyptic reassures that God is on the case. What appears to be defeat at every turn is in fact a preparation for the new age in which Christ's victory, already won, will be made manifest.

It is perhaps worth saying that although this method of reading the text is mainstream and widespread, there are those who do read this in a more literal way, or a way less defined by the contemporary situation of the addressees, and who use the book to interpret current events against an expectation of a series of interventions by God in our own time.

How can we use this material?

Perhaps the most accessible starting point is the letters to the seven churches. Seven may be a symbolic number, but the author does have pointed things to say in his review of each church, in a way which invites comparison with communities of faith today, reminding us that the issues surrounding communities of faith are not new.

Read 📖 *Revelation 2.1–7. Ephesus was an extremely cosmopolitan city where questions of religious definition and identity were important. This was also the centre for the worship of the goddess Diana, and a sizeable tourist industry had built up around pilgrimages, which proved a nice little earner that no one wanted disturbed. In this situation we read how Christians had endured this stressful context and had been rigorous about membership. But therein lies a problem. In being so concerned about maintaining purity they ran the risk of losing the very thing that gave them definition and identity – their love. Can you think of any similar situations? What advice would you give to those in Ephesus-like conditions?*

Or read 📖 *Revelation 2.18–29. The church at Thyatira was the first one in this list of seven to die out. Clearly it was very much at risk. This city was a great centre of trade, particularly to do with the cloth industry. It was a great place for belonging, apparently. Not to belong to a trade guild was commercial suicide, yet for Christians to belong might involve some compromises. The Guild meals, for example, used meat that had been sacrificed to idols. Can you think of situations today in which some Christians might run the risk of being compromised through belonging to organizations or societies that are important for their livelihoods?*

Chapters 4 and 5 might make more sense if you have read this chapter thus far.

Read 📖 *chapter 5, thinking of it as a fresh expression of the Gospel in a new idiom. What is different about this account? You might note the symbolism of the lamb – how effective is that do you think? You might note also the context of worship. Is the point here that Christian truth about God's victory is best understood and expressed in the community of faith at worship? What are the implications of this for churches that you might know? How attractive is this statement of faith for you?*

An interesting chapter for those who want a foothold in the real world while reading this book is 📖 *chapter 18. This is a lament over the demise of Babylon. It is the chapter where Babylon gets what's coming to it. Note particularly the number of references to trade and commerce. The fall of Babylon is not just about some ancient kingdom or empire. It is about the overthrow of a system that perhaps we can recognize. Do you see any connection between this description and the warnings that came after the Second World War about the rise of the industrial-military complex, for example?*

Finally, you might look at the picture of the new age. Read 📖 *Revelation 21.1–4, 22–27, 22.1–5. The age dawns in a context of worship, and yet the new Jerusalem contains no church. What conclusions do you draw from that? Note that this is not a picture of the end of the world or what happens to individuals after death, but rather a picture of a whole new creation: a new heaven and a new earth.*

The Bible has come full circle from creation to new creation, and in the process answered the question with which it began. God's grace will inevitably and finally prove stronger than human evil, corruption and sin. Goodness is stronger than evil. Love is the final arbiter of all things.

Afterword: What next?

Having got started, what next?

If you want a systematic way of reading the Bible on a daily basis, then get hold of a lectionary – a scheme of daily readings – selected passages from the Old Testament, the Psalms, the Epistles and the Gospels. The one most commonly used throughout the English-speaking world is the Revised Common Lectionary. The Church of England's Common Worship lectionary is based on this. There are organizations such as the Bible Reading Fellowship, Scripture Union and others that produce their own systematic series of readings together with commentary notes.

If you want to read more books, books about the Bible are of various kinds.

- Whole Bible commentaries give a chapter-by-chapter introduction to every book of the Bible and often include other explanatory or background articles. These are often revised, and usually contain solid scholarship.
- Commentaries on particular books that may interest you are usually available in series. The best bet is to find a series that speaks to you – not necessarily one that just ratifies your own views – and is not overly complicated by footnotes, jargon and small print. The Interpretation series, published by Westminster John Knox, is one I am usually happy to recommend.
- One-off books about Bible subjects are not good publishing bets, so publishers tend only to publish those written by

authors who have a following. In this case, first find your author, then read the books. Their bibliographies may well suggest other avenues.

If you want to join a Bible study group, they too come in various guises.

- Some groups are organized by educational establishments as part of an extramural programme. These have no necessary connection with any faith community, and your own faith history is not likely to be an issue.
- Some churches organize similar non-threatening groups, some of which are taught and some primarily for discussion. Sometimes there is a course book, the initial perusal of which should give you an idea of whether it's for you. Often these courses operate just during Lent. Sometimes they have a longer programme, perhaps following a reading club agenda, or using material such as the *Church Times Study Guides* series.
- Some churches run 'nurture courses', whose aim is both to inform and to inspire or persuade. There is nothing sinister in this and you can opt out at any point. The plus in this kind of group is that actually the best people to talk about faith are people for whom faith means something. These too, often have a course handbook.
- Churches also sometimes run Bible groups where the aim is not so much to teach and inform, but rather to share insights and experience. Visits to local churches will soon give you a sense of whether, in such a context, your mind will meet others.

You will soon come to know the authors, the publishers and the contexts that actually feed you.

Of course, it is possible to follow degree courses in Theology, majoring on the Bible, and these can usually be achieved in a modular course over a period of amassing credits. Local universities or the Open University can furnish more details.

Most of all, enjoy your reading. Don't make a chore out of it and remember that the Bible's main context is a community of faith.